RESTORING
THE
Beauty

ALSO BY STEVE HARRISON

Consuming Love *Liberating Love* *Suffering Love* *The Clash of Kingdoms*

Available today from Ardor Media
https://kingsroadministries.com

P.O. Box 320
Brainerd, MN 56401

Ardor Media is a division of Bethany Urban Development, a ministry dedicated
to promoting transforming revivals in urban communities.

STEVE HARRISON

RESTORING
THE
Beauty

HELPING MEN GAIN AND SUSTAIN
VICTORY **OVER** SEXUAL SIN

Publisher: Ardor Media

P.O. Box 320

Brainerd, MN 56401

ISBN: 979-8-9911792-1-8 (softcover)

ISBN: 979-8-9911792-0-1 (eBook)

First printing: 2024

Printed in the United States of America

DEDICATION

I would like to dedicate this book to the thousands of men and women in faith-based treatment centers throughout the world. You desire more than sobriety; you seek character excellence that honors God. May all His plans and purposes for your life be fulfilled!

ACKNOWLEDGEMENTS

Daniel Harrison, Dillon Forest, Micah Norby for their insights and input.

Cover design: Sheryl Thornberg for your skill in conveying words into art. This is our fourth project together. What an incredible gift God has given you. I just love working with you.

Ronald Olson, for your courageous and precise editing. I so appreciated your insight and assistance. You made the rough edges smooth.

The team from Believers Book Services. Thanks, Dave Sheets, for keeping everything moving forward. You were always so helpful and encouraging.

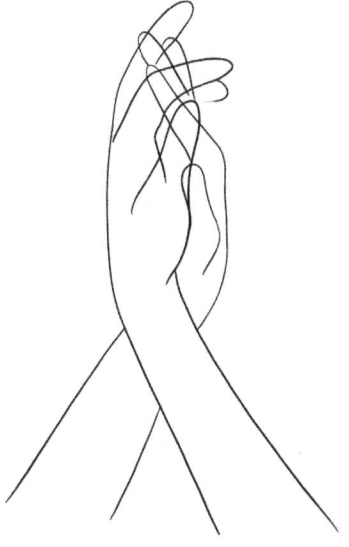

TABLE OF CONTENTS

1. Pyromania 1

2. Spiritual Arson 13

3. Excavation 25

4. Implementation 43

5. Restoration 57

6. Reinforcement 69

7. Fireproofing 83

FOREWORD

"On and on . . . and still on!"

If you're anything like me, your email inbox is inundated weekly with ministry emails, updates and other messages from a plethora of people, most of which are shallow and get instantly deleted. One notable exception in my case is anytime I receive one from my old friend, Steve Harrison. I almost always immediately drop everything I am doing and settle in for a focused read and some prayerful reflection time.

Why? Because in every case, his short messages seem to come right from the throne room of God. They contain potent truth; packaged with Steve's unique flavor of personal examples, scripture, quotes from various believers from salvation-history and relevant insights.

So, when I was asked to write the Foreword for his new book, I had to pray about it—for exactly five seconds—before answering an enthusiastic, "YES!" I knew his book would be an extension of the anointing contained in his wonderful ministry emails. I have not been disappointed.

This book is spiritual dynamite. I found myself having to stop reading quite often, and just sit to ponder and let the truth I was receiving sink in. And this book is timely, especially with sexual sins and sexual brokenness running rampant in our culture. This current generation seems to be playing on a field with no boundaries.

This book is deeply scriptural, filled with truth, and through the thought-provoking study questions at the end of every chapter, very practical. So, if ever we needed a book like this, it's now.

Here are three words to leave with you as you begin the wonderful adventure of digging into this book.

REALITIES

Be prepared to feel challenged as Steve lays out scripture upon scripture to help reveal that God's fields DO have necessary boundaries, especially when it comes to our sexuality as human beings. We are the crowning jewel of His creation and are made as close to God Himself as anything He created.

Feeling challenged can lead to new realities in your life, if you are ready to partner with the Holy Spirit and instill the new disciplines that are required.

One of Steve's quotes that struck me so deeply on this subject is this:

"Notice that humans were the only thing in God's creation that were not created by His word, but only by His hands. He quickly demonstrated that He was willing to get His hands dirty for us. It is because He wanted to be more intimately involved in our creation and our ongoing lives."

Created by His hands! Wow!

I was personally challenged on multiple fronts throughout many chapters, and I had to stop and pray that the guidelines that Steve was laying out would become greater realities in my own life.

REVELATION

Throughout Steve's writings, we catch a glimpse of a man who continually is hearing from God and encouraging us of the need to *"go and do likewise."*

Hearing God's voice is a subject that is dear to my heart. In this book you will catch yourself in moments of reflection as Steve intimately shares actual revelation that came to him directly from the mouth and heart of God in different moments of his life.

These revelatory thoughts form a framework within the scriptural foundations and biblical references. They will encourage you to dig deeper in your relationship with the Father. Through deeper relationship comes victory over temptations, along with obedience and wholeness.

As Steve so aptly puts it, *I believe there is a correlation between hearing God's voice and our willingness to obey. If we are not hearing God's voice, it could be because we haven't obeyed the last thing He told us to do. Obedience opens the door of communication with God.*

RESTORATION

I suppose I am borrowing from a key word in the title of this book, but this theme came so strongly to me, and I know you will likewise be inspired by it.

God's ways are always FOR us. His plan of redemption through the cross gives us the foundation of truth that He is working (even when we don't see it or perceive it) to restore His Creation to something beautiful!

What if you could wake up tomorrow feeling renewed, loved deeply, eternally secure in your identity as a son or daughter of the King of kings? What if you were restored in body, soul and spirit from the presence of the Holy Spirit?

YOU CAN!

To quote Steve a third time:

The Lord said clearly, "I am restoring the beauty!" This was profound to me. I always knew of God's forgiving heart and a willingness to wash us clean. This, however, was beyond my current understanding.

What God seemed to be saying was that He was not satisfied with forgiveness of our sins. He wanted a restoration of innocence and a renewed perspective of sex. I saw He wanted to heal and restore—not just forgive. His goal is restoration. He wants us to be able to look at others the way He does.

Reading this book, discussing the various themes with a trusted friend, answering honestly the questions at the end of each chapter, and then praying through the truths you have learned, can lead you to a restoration of the beauty of God's gift of sexuality.

To close, here's one of my favorite quotes that Steve utilizes. It's from William Booth, founder of the Salvation Army,

So, hurry to the rescue, lift up your heads, fix your eyes on the future, rise to your opportunities, the biggest and grandest and most pregnant with blessing of any that have come to anyone in these last days. Forget the failures of the past, leave them behind you, let the devil have them, and having taken your stand, then . . . on and on . . . and still on.

Rev. Carl Wesley Anderson

Equipping Evangelist and Founder of Born to Blaze Ministries

Author/Documentary Filmmaker of the book and TV Series, *Love Speaks: 21 Ways to Recognize God's Multi-Faceted Voice.*

INTRODUCTION

When I decided to give my life to Christ in the summer of 1972, a young Christian man challenged me to give up everything that had come between me and the Lord. I wrote out a list that included a 1970 454 Chevelle, a Honda motorcycle, and a girlfriend. It also included the recreational drugs that I had grown fond of. He told me to take that list in one hand and imagine Jesus in the other hand. I needed to choose which one I would serve.

That night, I knelt at an old-fashioned altar at a youth camp in northern Minnesota. In doing so, I had made the decision to turn away from my sins and everything on that list. God immediately transformed my heart, and I knew I was never going back to my old way of life. Surprisingly, letting it all go was not that difficult. I sold my Chevelle for $2500, even though today it would be worth more than thirty times that amount. I sold my Honda and broke up with my girlfriend. I got rid of my drugs, and I have never used again.

It all makes for a wonderful testimony except for one small detail—sexual lust. To my surprise, this did not disappear like the rest. As a Christian, I found this part of my life continued to oppress and distract me. I wanted to be free from all sins, but this one refused to die. Fast forward fifty years. I now find myself discipling a group of Christian men, many of whom are new believers. Sexual lust has emerged as the battle of their lives as well. No one is comfortable talking about it, but very few seem to be experiencing sustained victory over it. God has saved and restored our lives, but we seem willing to burn it all down to gratify our sexual lusts. The problem is too large for this book alone to solve. I only hope to provide practical and spiritual insights to help you in your battle over sexual sin.

Recently, God shared with me that He was looking for those who had the tongue of a prophet and a heart of a pastor. That is my goal. I want to speak the truth in love (Ephesians 4:15). After you read this book, I would strongly recommend that you discuss the contents with someone else. It will give you encouragement and boldness to apply what the Holy Spirit reveals to you. May God give you strength to be Christ-like in all areas of weakness, so that nothing will delay God's plans and purposes for you.

Chapter 1

PYROMANIA

Pyromania: an impulse control disorder in which individuals repeatedly fail to resist impulses to deliberately start fires, to relieve some tension or for instant gratification.[1] For years our culture has been fanning the flames of sexual gratification, while ignoring the destructive consequences of doing so. As a result, we are being consumed by the fire of sexual desire.

Therefore God gave them over in the sinful desires of their hearts to sexual impurity for the degrading of their bodies with one another.

ROMANS 1:24

SHE CRIED

I'm an ordinary guy—younger than some, older than most. It seems every man has a story. You know what I'm talking about—that unforgettable sexual encounter. I will tell you mine.

I grew up in a small town, and when I was eleven years old a friend of mine from the big city came to visit. Since our parents knew each other, my friend was able to stay for an entire week. He was two years older than me, which made him older than most of the neighborhood kids.

One day he asked me about one of the neighborhood girls. "Have you ever had sex with her?"

"What? Of course not. She's my neighbor," I replied.

"I think I could get her in bed," he said confidently.

"No way," was my response.

It wasn't long before he approached her for a date. She said, "Yes." Now the plan was set. My friend was going to sneak out of our house to see her and return later that night.

I felt anxious as he left and couldn't wait for him to return. Finally, around 10:30 p.m., he snuck back without my parents' knowledge. Immediately, I asked him how it went. He boasted it went well. Then I asked him the all-important question, "Did you go to bed with her?"

"Yes," he said.

I was completely shocked. As my mind was short-circuiting, I continued, "Well, what did she do?"

He paused for a moment and then said the words I will never forget.

"She cried."

Recently, the song "Don't Make Her Cry" was released by my friends, Buddy and Julie Miller. The song was based on the words Regina McCrary's father, Reverend Sam McCrary, said to Bob Dylan when they met at a Nashville show in 1978, shortly after she joined Dylan's band.[2] Reverend McCrary's sentiment echoed what every concerned father would have for their precious child. It is also the sentiment our Heavenly Father has for every precious child that He knows and cares for.

The experience with the neighbor girl was not the first time I felt conflicted with our culture's sexual beliefs. When I was a preteen, an older neighbor boy first told me about masturbation. I was surprised by his instructions and advice. He said, "Don't do it too much or it could become a problem." It wasn't long before I awkwardly tried it for the first time. What he didn't warn me about was how uneasy I would feel afterwards. In the absence of any human influence, I felt guilty and unclean. I'll never forget that initial impression.

These sexual conflicts were the last thing I felt comfortable talking about. I'm not alone. Most men want to avoid these issues like the plague. It is a big reason why this problem is not being adequately addressed. But I can't get certain concerns and fears out of my mind. Since my childhood sexual experiences, I have seen more than my share of hurt and pain caused by the selfish use of sex. I believe sex outside of marriage has caused more tears than any other vice in this world. I may be wrong, but I don't think so. Madison Avenue tells us that sex sells. You won't get an argument from me. But let's be honest, they mostly fail to tell you sex costs a lot.

America may be leading the way when it comes to marketing sex, but she is not alone. A few years ago, I flew to Paris. As I got off the plane, I was struck by the number of seductive advertising signs in the airport. In my spirit I heard, "They worship the female form."

Perhaps that's what it has come down to. We don't just tolerate sex; we have become obsessed with it. It is a god that demands and receives our worship. Jonathan Cahn once wrote, "When Israel turned away from God, sex, in the form of the goddess Ashtoreth, or Ishtar, was deified. Sex became a god. Sex thus became an end and a goal to be pursued in and of itself."[3] There have been various campaigns to educate the public on the dangers of smoking and overdrinking. When was the last time there was a serious campaign about the costly effects of sex outside of marriage?

Besides the advertising industry, some blame our sexual obsessiveness on the devil or our sinful nature. Others think it is because of this world's system, particularly the entertainment industry. Movies tell us a story. What is the basic plot in most? A man is on a quest that is delayed or altered because of his sexual neediness. The James Bond movies are a good example of this. So are many superhero movies. Recently, more of these movies portray women as superior because they don't appear to have this weakness.

I'm not a fan of horror movies but I have noticed another common plot. A man is seduced by a beautiful woman. As she embraces him seductively, the woman suddenly transforms into her real self, which happens to be an ugly, demonic figure who instantly and violently destroys the man. Sadly, this is a more realistic portrayal of sex's dangerous disguise.

Whoever is to blame for our over-sexed culture, we are continually faced with contradictory messages. It reminds me of watching a Popeye cartoon where he eats spinach to get stronger, all the while smoking a corncob pipe. We are educated on the importance of sensitivity, honor and respect, but at the same time we are encouraged to be flirtatious and seductive. We have the MeToo movement against the backdrop of increased sexually explicit images in the media. We hear claims of misogyny and sexual harassment, while OnlyFans becomes the latest cultural trend. We live in a culture that encourages us to be sexually irresistible, while maintaining a "look but don't touch" policy. Our adult heads are spinning, while our teenagers are losing theirs.

It didn't use to be so confusing. There was a day when most people had views that were close to a biblical standard. But all that has changed. Recently, I read a story of a TV weatherman who lived a double life as an adult film actor. When this became public, he was let go from the television station. To find new employment, he hired an agency that specializes in rebuilding their client's reputation. In defense of the weatherman, a spokesman supported him by saying, "I think it's a different generation out there. I think younger people just don't care about these kinds of things; it's not an issue. I think when you talk about people under forty, virtual sex and nude photos are pretty much part of the life."[4]

Years ago, the Reagan administration rolled out an antidrug program called, "Just Say No." It didn't work and has since become a pop culture joke. It takes more than a simple statement to undo years of cultural influence. The same is true with sex. We have been groomed to accept sex outside of marriage, self-pleasuring, and sexual entertainment as reasonable human rights. It will take a lot to undo this programming.

A TRIP IN TIME

During the COVID crisis, we constantly heard the mantra, "Follow the Science." The point was to look objectively at the scientific data in making public policy. Let's take this to another level, and this time "Follow the History." I believe if we honestly and objectively study our past, we should be better equipped to direct our future. Perhaps a little history can help get our heads screwed on right.

The French Revolution was a period of major social upheaval that began in 1789 and ended in 1799. When we think of this historical event, we often have images of the guillotine, Marie Antoinette, and the overthrow of the French monarchy. However, there was much more going on beneath the surface. According to author and social critic Os Guinness, the French Revolution was a sexual revolution, a revolution not based on biblical values but upon militant secularism. During this time, French society was casting off moral values and everything considered repressive. Some of these "enlightened" views were:

1. Humans are essentially good, and only need to be freed from sexual repressions to be happy.

2. Sexual permissiveness will produce the greatest human freedom.

3. Gender identity can be decided by subjective feelings.

4. Naturalistic science is adequate to answer all the questions of life.

5. Two decisive sources of repression are the monogamous family and religion, especially the Jewish and Christian faiths.

6. Sexual repression should be removed at the youngest age.

7. No form of sexual relations of any kind should be prohibited.

8. Absolutely nothing must be allowed to stand in the way of the freedom of the sexual revolution.[5]

Does any of this sound strangely familiar? Did throwing off sexual restraint produce a new utopia for the French people? Hardly. Despite the tragic results, all of these measures have gained popularity in the United States for the past fifty years. Do you think we will be successful where the French failed? Remember the saying, "Insanity is doing the same thing over and over and expecting different results." But let's broaden our research a bit to gain additional understanding.

FATE OF EMPIRES

Several years ago, I discovered an insightful essay on world history. *The Fate of Empires* was a broad study involving eleven major empires (superpowers) over the past 4,000 years. These included Assyria, Persia, Greece, Roman Republic, Roman Empire, Arab Empire, Mamluk Empire, Ottoman Empire, Spain, Romanov Russia, and Britain. Interestingly, the book of Daniel speaks extensively about three of these empires: Persia, Greece, and Rome.

According to the research, each empire made a unique and massive impact on the world. Ironically, they all had an average life span of 250 years before disappearing from the world stage.[6] Also, surprising, was that they all went through six stages of development.

Stage One (The Age of Pioneers): These people were poor, but highly motivated. Because of their extraordinary energy and courage, they often overthrew decaying empires.

Stage Two (The Age of Conquests): This was a time of military expansion.

As a result, there were increases in communication, commerce, and exploration.

Stage Three (The Age of Commerce): During this stage, the desire to make money transcended the desire for military glory. Profitable enterprises began to spring up.[7]

Stage Four (The Age of Affluence): There was a decline in courage and sense of duty. Education became the means for higher salaries, and defensiveness replaced expansion.[8]

Stage Five (The Age of Intellect): Academic honors replaced the pursuit of adventure and military glory. People believed human intellect could solve the problems of the world. They developed a sense of superiority.[9]

Stage Six (The Age of Decadence): This final stage contained several unique characteristics:

- Intensification of political hatreds
- Influx of foreigners
- Frivolity – celebrity worship (singers, athletes, and actors)[10]
- A welfare state
- Decline in religion[11]
- Reversal of sexes. Increased number of women in the workplace
- Abandonment of sexual morality[12]

We need to pause and let this sink in. Then we need to ask ourselves some hard questions. Which of these stages would best describe our current culture? Assuming that the United States is the 12th superpower, how close are we to the average 250-year life span? Considering what has happened repeatedly in the past, is there any question about the danger we are facing? These are sobering considerations, but perhaps we could use a bit more historical proof.

SEX AND CULTURE

I would like to submit a landmark study by ethnologist and social anthropologist J. D. Unwin. The 700-page *Sex and Culture* was first published in 1934. This was not a religious study. Unwin studied eighty primitive tribes and six known civilizations through 5,000 years of history. He sought the answer to one single question: Does a culture's ideas of sexual liberation predict its success or collapse? What he discovered was profound.

To be more specific:

• When there were sexual restraints, both before and during marriage, the culture always flourished. However, total sexual freedom always led to the collapse of the culture within three generations.

• The single most determining factor in a culture flourishing or collapsing was its view of sex before marriage. A culture is successful to the extent that it restricts prenuptial sex.

• The most powerful combination was chastity before marriage and monogamy in marriage. Cultures that retained this combination for at least three generations exceeded all other cultures in every area, including art, science, and agriculture.[13]

Unwin concluded that the whole of human history does not contain a single instance of a group becoming civilized unless it has been absolutely monogamous, nor is there any example of a group retaining its culture after it has adopted less rigorous customs.[14]

WE'RE SCREWED

In the 1960s, our generation embraced a sexual revolution. New verbiage seemed to appear out of nowhere like "right of privacy" and "consensual sex." Along with recreational drugs, we initially felt it would usher in the Age of Aquarius. After numerous unwanted children and countless casualties from drugs, the optimism began to fade. But the genie was out of the bottle. Now, sixty years later, Generation Z represents the critical third generation Unwin described.

Sadly, if all these historical facts were universally known and accepted, we probably still would not do anything about it. Sometimes, I want to cry. After all, few seem to have the courage or will to challenge the current status quo. We are in a moral malaise unprecedented in our history, and we are just accepting it. As a member of the baby boomer generation, I want to apologize for ever embracing more sexual freedom. As a lost teenager, I thought it would be a positive change. Now that it is normalized, we are paying a high price for our low living.

It reminds me of a road rage driver who rammed another vehicle and set her own car on fire by furiously revving her engine. Ironically, a nearby good Samaritan tried to free her, but as he testified:

> "I opened the driver's door wide. It opened easily. The person looked at me. I said 'You've got to get out of the car. It's going to burst into flames.' But she raised her right fist towards me in a threatening manner before slamming the door shut. I was a bit bewildered and moved three to four yards back. I could see her gesturing towards me. She seemed to be in quite a rage. Both fists were raised and being shaken, and the person was looking right at me. This was definitely done in a manner to tell me to stay away from her car."

> The good Samaritan ran to his workshop and fetched a fire extinguisher. He used it on the car, but it had no effect. Someone else also had an extinguisher but that made no difference either. The heat got more and more intense while the flames grew. They no longer could see the woman inside. When the fire department was finally able to extinguish the blaze, it was clear the woman inside was already dead.[15]

The woman was clearly in danger, but she ignored the signs. She was given every opportunity to escape, yet she refused because she was determined to keep going in the direction she was headed. Likewise, our current culture has become blind and obstinate regarding sexual freedom.

In 2022, Louise Perry wrote *The Case Against the Sexual Revolution*. This tour de force so thoroughly decimates any case for the sexual revolution that hardly a shred is left standing.[16] Perry is a nonreligious feminist who has exposed the lies regarding sexual freedom in our culture. Some of her recent findings reveal:

• Today's young women are typically unaware that men are, in general, much better suited to emotionless sex and find it much easier to regard their sexual partners as disposable. Ignorant of this fact, women can all too easily fail to recognize that being desired is not at all the same thing as being held in high esteem.[17]

• Porn trains the mind to regard sex as a spectator sport, to be enjoyed alone and in front of a screen. It removes love and mutuality from sex, turning human beings . . . into body parts.[18]

• If we try and pretend that sex has no special value that makes it different from other acts, then we end up in some very dark places. If sex isn't worthy of its own moral category, then neither is sexual harassment nor rape.[19]

There's a very short and brutal poem by the Scottish poet Hollie McNish, "Conversation With An Archeologist," which served as an epigraph for the abovementioned book.

> "He said they'd found a brothel
> On the dig he did last night
> I asked him how they know
> He sighed:
> a pit of babies' bones
> a pit of newborn babies' bones was how to spot a brothel."[20]

In excavating ancient Roman sites, first you find the erotic statuary, then you dig a bit more and find the male infant skeletons. Male of course, because males were of no use to the keepers of Roman brothels, whereas the female infants born to prostituted women were raised into prostitution themselves.[21]

REFLECTION AND DISCUSSION

Have you witnessed or experienced sexual abuse? In what ways has it affected you?

_____

_____

_____

Why do you think our culture is filled with mixed messages on sex?

_____

_____

_____

Which of the "enlightened" views of the French Revolution pose the greatest threat to our society?

_____

_____

_____

Which of the six stages mentioned in Fate of Empires would best describe our current culture?

_____

_____

_____

In Sex and Culture, it mentions the most powerful combination for a culture was chastity before marriage and monogamy in marriage. Is this achievable in our country? Why?

_____

_____

_____

Do you agree with Louise Perry's conclusion in _The Case Against the Sexual Revolution?_ Why?_____

_____

_____

_____

Chapter 2

SPIRITUAL ARSON

Negligent arson or reckless burning involves the intentional act of starting a fire or setting fire to something with a disregard for the potential consequences.[1] Our negligence and recklessness have created the moral morass we are in. We can't blame it on the devil or the world. The Church needs to take responsibility for the spiritual condition of our world.

Take no part in the worthless deeds of evil and darkness; instead, expose them.

EPHESIANS 5:11

"HOUSTON, WE HAVE A PROBLEM"

Those famous words were uttered by the crew of Apollo 13 when they faced a life-threatening malfunction on their historic trip to the moon in 1970. Throughout the tense ordeal, they continued to speak and think professionally. It has become a cultural cliché to describe an ironic understatement.

I have been teaching a discipleship class for young Christian men for over ten years. A while back, I asked them a simple question, "When it comes to sexual integrity, what is your greatest struggle?" This was their response.

1. Mine is porn. I try to not do it, but I fail a lot of times.

2. Masturbation, thoughts.

3. Greatest struggle for me is definitely masturbation. Still working on overcoming it.

4. Lusting thoughts toward women.

5. Sex before marriage, always expecting sex.

6. I would have to say the easy ability to go get laid whenever I want.

7. Looking at women as sexual objects and sex outside of wedlock because it seems like that nowadays starts relationships.

8. Having sex without being married.

9. Keeping the act of sexual intimacy sacred (just with one—as in marriage).

10. I would say the sexual desire for pleasure. So, I struggle with everything that comes with this topic and it's an everyday battle for me.

11. Not caring who I hurt when I am with a woman. My lusting for women, looking at them, and talking about them.

Sadly, no one, not one person, expressed victory in this area. Based on this simple survey, do you think we might have a problem in the Church today? In the past several years, I have worked in the recovery community. In thousands of counseling sessions, this keeps coming up again and again. What I have discovered is that sexual sin is THE gateway drug—more than alcohol, cigarettes, and marijuana. It is the elephant in the room. Quite frankly, I am shocked the Church has not done more for those hopelessly addicted to porn, masturbation, and the inability to see others except through the prism of sexual gratification.

SHEPHERD SCANDALS

For the past fifty years, I have been working as a Christian minister. I can say confidently that sexual sin has ruined more ministries and churches than anything else I know. During this time, I have had to deal with several sexual scandals—not just with those outside of the Church, but many within. According to a recent Barna study, 68% of church-going men and over 50% of pastors view porn on a regular basis. Of young Christian adults 18 to 24 years old, 76% actively search for porn.[2]

To my amazement and disappointment, many Christian leaders have chosen to become involved in extramarital affairs. Many others are currently losing a daily battle with porn and lust. In their effort to cover their sin, these leaders often become pretentious and manipulative. They attempt to defuse people's suspicions and questions by controlling the narrative. I have seen those under them thrown into chaos, hurt, and uncertainty because of their leaders' failures. I agree with pastor and author, JC Groves who said, "You. No matter who you are. No matter how long you've been in ministry. No matter how big or small the ministry is. You are one decision away from stupid. One decision away from ruining it all. Don't be a statistic."[3]

I once worked with an influential Christian ministry for several years. We were surrounded with incredibly dedicated ministers and staff workers who sacrificed all for the sake of expanding God's Kingdom. It was inconceivable to me that any of our leaders would become involved in a sexual scandal, but that's what happened. More than once. It crushed the hope and optimism so many of us enjoyed. How could the leadership fail to uphold the same biblical standards they so often demanded? There were other factors involved as well, but these scandals were mortal wounds in our ministry.

Fast forward a few years. I was serving on the board of a small but strategic ministry. Suddenly, we discovered that the founder and leader had been texting explicit messages to an underage girl in another state. The leader was immediately removed, but the damage was done. This leader refused to adhere to the discipline meted out by the board and chose to reorganize the ministry with the support of his local church. What a mess.

I've recently discovered what appears to be sexual abuse between a friend of mine and a major Christian leader. It breaks my heart. When will this stop? I hate to say it, but you start to wonder if sexual scandals will destroy the Western Church's ability to be a godly influence in our culture. I am not a prophet or son of a prophet, but it doesn't take any special anointing to see what is going on. To not see it, our head would have to be buried in the sand. Unfortunately, that's what many have chosen to do.

OUR ACHILLES' HEEL

The Western Church's tolerance of sexual sin has become our Achilles' heel. We may pray for revival. We may think we deserve God's blessings and favor, but let's be honest. Is that a legitimate expectation when we are harboring major sexual sins we refuse to confess and repent from?

Recently, a Christian brother described a dangerous trend. Christians often promote themselves on social media, while having a great time. Tragically, these "great times" can involve an exotic vacation or weekend camping trip with a girlfriend. If that wasn't bad enough, many Christians send them "likes" or some congratulatory comment like, "I'm so happy for you guys," or "y'all are such a cute couple." Rarely do you see any Christian challenge their behavior.

I believe many single Christian adults would date non-Christians. According to Pew Research in 2020, 50% of Christian adults say casual sex is sometimes or always acceptable.[4] Many would go on a camping trip or vacation cruise with a girlfriend. Many think these things are wrong, but like a Christian friend once said, "I know it's wrong, but all I have to do is ask God for forgiveness afterwards."

In the Bible, there is a story of Amnon who was King David's firstborn. He was the presumptive heir to the throne and enjoyed a life of power and privilege. However, he had a weakness. He was a man obsessed with the beauty of a certain woman named Tamar (see 2 Samuel 13). What made it complicated was that she was his half sister. Despite this, he couldn't control his sexual obsession for her. Finally, Amnon shared his predicament with his friend, Jonadab, who helped him hatch a sinister plan.

Amnon pretended to be sick and asked that Tamar serve him breakfast in bed. When she innocently did so, he grabbed her and raped her. Amazingly, after the assault, Amnon's heart turned against Tamar. The Bible states, *Then Amnon hated her with intense hatred. In fact, he hated her more than he had loved her* (2 Samuel 13:15). The passage clearly demonstrates that Amnon never truly loved Tamar—he only lusted after her. That's the irony of lust. It is often disguised as intense love. Tragically, what God intended to be an act of unselfish love, often becomes extremely selfish and cruel.

I've been a witness to the spiritually corrosive power of sexual sin. Men and women, on fire for God, suddenly become emotionally cold and spiritually lukewarm. Something dies inside of them. Spiritual truths no longer inspire them. They no longer have vision or moral clarity. They are in a perpetual moral fog. I have seen it in their eyes. There is a disconnect with God that leaves the person spiritually dull and lethargic. They have become a shell of what they once were. Often, common sense advice and reminders of their former self fall on deaf ears. They have sunk into a dark pit and lack the strength or motivation to get out. It is painfully frustrating to see this happen to coworkers who were once powerfully used by God.

OUR DIRTY LITTLE SECRET

Everyone knows the story of Moses and the ten plagues of Egypt. Shortly after, the Lord delivered the Children of Israel from the hand of Pharaoh by dividing the Red Sea. After their successful crossing, they made their way to Mt. Sinai. It was there that Moses went up the mountain to meet with God and receive the Ten Commandments. While on the summit, his brother Aaron, the chief priest, was put in charge of the people. Tragically, Aaron soon facilitated blatant idolatry and pagan revelry. He compromised his spiritual leadership. When Moses saw the moral debauchery and compromise, he asked a question that continues to echo through the Western Church, *"Who is on the Lord's side?"* (Exodus 32:25-30).

In the Old Testament, God wanted to establish integrity in the young Hebrew nation—a people who were set apart. They balked at the concept and demanded, *"We want to be like the nations around us"* (1 Samuel 8:20 NLT). As a result, God's people started adopting the foreign gods of the many nations surrounding them. Despite the clear warnings from God, they were continually drawn into idolatry. Their idolatry led to immorality. Their loss of respect for God led to a loss of respect for each other.

God's people were enticed by gods and religions that tolerated and even encouraged sexual immorality. This was a constant challenge for Moses, Joshua, and Nehemiah. After initial victories in the Promised Land, God's people soon lost their ability to drive out their enemies because of their moral corruption. Their failures serve as a warning of the serious consequences awaiting any of God's people who act in the same way, and a clarion call to restore moral integrity and holiness.

God frequently used the metaphor of sexual immorality to describe His people's spiritual condition. This is the theme of the book of Hosea. *Prostitution, wine, and new wine take away the mind and the [spiritual] understanding. My people consult their [lifeless] wooden idol, and their [diviner's] wand gives them oracles. For a spirit of prostitution has led them astray [morally and spiritually], And they have played the prostitute, withdrawing themselves from their God* (Hosea 4:11-12 AMP). Later, in the New Testament, God uses marital unfaithfulness as a metaphor to describe the depth of His hurt and sense of betrayal. *You adulterous people, don't you know that friendship with the world means enmity against God? Therefore, anyone who chooses to be a friend of the world becomes an enemy of God* (James 4:4).

About 120 years ago, a charismatic movement began worldwide that led to a rediscovery of spiritual gifts and a deep passion for holiness. Slowly, over the years, this movement lost its focus on holiness. Attention to success (as our culture defines it) became more common. Many churches within the movement began to abandon their spiritual roots as new measures were introduced. In their efforts to reach the world, they tried to become more *like* the world. I believe this has affected even the way we worship. Call me a killjoy, but I believe there is a sensual spirituality starting to infect our worship.

Recently, I was introduced to the term "romantic worship." The line between spirituality and sensuality is thinner than many realize. Christian music videos are often entertainment driven. Sex sells in the world, and it is easy to convey that vibe. People are tempted by those possessed with extraordinary beauty, singing passionately about love. More videos seem to cater to the world at the very least, and sensual arousal at worst. Years ago, David Wilkerson prophesied that in the future, nudity would be allowed in church. I thought it was impossible, but now it seems much more plausible.

SEX WITHOUT HONOR

God created sex, and in its proper context, it is beautiful. In fact, it is very beautiful. But something else is beautiful in the Bible, and that is honor. Honor is a major theme in Scripture, and you find it clearly in the Ten Commandments. The first four are about honoring God. The fifth one is about honoring your parents. The remaining five are all about honoring your neighbor or community. Jesus constantly sought to honor His Father. He saw the beauty and value in everyone, especially those who were vulnerable and hurting.

Honor must be a guiding principle in our lives, especially regarding something as sacred as sex. *Do you not know that your bodies are temples of the Holy Spirit, who is in you, whom you have received from God? You are not your own; you were bought at a price. Therefore **honor God with your bodies*** (1 Corinthians 6:19-20 emphasis mine).

The problem today is that we have sex without honor. As a result, people have been hurt. No, let me rephrase that. People have been devastated because someone sexually exploited them. I can't think of anything that damages the deepest parts of a human soul more than this.

Have you ever walked into a store and noticed a woman dressed in provocative clothing? One time, the Lord gave me a different perspective of a woman doing this. I began to consider the desire we all have for attention and approval. For some, to dress sexy is a popular means to obtain that. The problem is, the message seems to be picked up primarily by those driven by untamed sexual desires. The result is that the person wearing provocative clothing ultimately is deceived and often abused by them. This results in deeper hurt, insecurity, and shame.

What if we could simply, *Love each other as brothers and sisters* (1 Peter 3:8 NLT)? Imagine if we lived our lives to make others feel honored and respected. Picture what could happen if we made this a goal with God, with our spouses, and those struggling with lack of self-respect and value.

ROAD TO INEVITABLE JUDGMENT?

Has the genie been let out of the bottle, never to return? Based on examples in Scripture, there is a possibility of delayed judgment—if the people would repent and pray. Through the preaching of Jonah, Ninevah was spared impending judgment (see Jonah 3:10). God even delayed judgment with King Ahab when he responded to a word of warning (see 1 Kings 21:25-29). Because of King Josiah's moral reforms, the Lord said, *"Your eyes will not see all the disaster I am going to bring on this place and on those who live here"* (2 Chronicles 34:28).

In all these cases, someone had a change of perspective and did something about it. They all had an "aha" moment when they saw something that they hadn't seen before. It was divine revelation brought about through the power of the Holy Spirit. This is the need of our hour.

Chapter Two

WAILING WALL

In Jerusalem there is a famous religious site called the Wailing Wall. The wall was originally constructed in the days of Solomon. Over the years, numerous religious buildings have been built and then destroyed, including the temple. However, a surviving part of ancient Israel is this section of wall that protected the original city of David.

In the book of Ezekiel, there are detailed instructions on guarding the city. It describes watchmen that were assigned to the top of this wall. Their job was to sound the alarm if danger drew near. There were strict penalties if they were negligent or irresponsible. Amid our current moral descent, watchmen must sound the alarm. Those who are privy to danger must warn others of what is coming. If they don't, they will bear the blame for the consequences. It's like a forest ranger who spots a fire from his tower but fails to warn the people in the fire's path.

It's time we got our heads out of the sand, hoping the problem will just go away. If we find humor in sexual jokes, then there is probably an unhealthy tolerance to sexual sin. It's time to stop minimizing and justifying. If we can't, then we are still part of the problem. *Let there be no sexual immorality, impurity, or greed among you. Such sins have no place among God's people. Obscene stories, foolish talk, and coarse jokes—these are not for you. Instead, let there be thankfulness to God. You can be sure that no immoral, impure, or greedy person will inherit the Kingdom of Christ and of God* (Ephesians 5:3-5 NLT).

We've got to get serious. God will not deliver us in an area of our lives we still find attractive. Either we tolerate sexual sin and remain hopelessly trapped, or we hate sexual sin and join with God as freedom fighters. We desperately need faithful watchmen who will sound the alarm with brokenness and love. The Church needs the protection of a wailing wall.

As a family, I remember going through a season of soul-searching several years ago. During that time, my daughter wrote a poem that has continued to be a reminder of our desperate need for God's grace and revelation. I beg you. I plead with you. Don't be a part of this problem. That is not your God-intended legacy. Don't yield to the cultural pressures of our day. Don't become another shipwrecked soul on the rocky shore of sexual compromise and addiction. A million times, "NO!"

Revive Us, Oh Lord

Dear Jesus, what have we become?
We are lifeless bones, our spirit numb.
We have one foot out and one foot in.
We denounce others but shelve our sin.
Our prayers have turned to tearless duty,
With no sincerity, and no beauty.
Oh, what anguished tears you weep.
To see your people fast asleep.
Our fires quenched; our passions gone.
Your beloved's lost her first love song.
And as hell devours in its mouth.
Thousands who are crying out.
Can we dare awaken to answer this?
Less deny what our commission is.
Is what we are living for worth your blood shed?
Or do we shamelessly dishonor your brutal death?
Let us fall to our knees. Let us turn now!
Let us cry out in the midnight hours!
Revive us oh Lord; make us never the same.
Take us through your raging flames.
Shatter our shells of pride and thoughtless mind.
Melt our hardened hearts with your precious love divine.
Let rivers of living water flow instead of pools of sin.
Purge out all the darkened shadows hidden deep within.
Oh Jesus, that we'd see again your tear-stained broken face.
Would we still try to justify? Would we try to plead our case?
Or would our eyes meet yours and cry out, "There is my first love!"
Being reminded once again that you alone are enough.
And at that moment die to self and all of our desires,
To be eternally set ablaze by your all-consuming fire.

MOLLY HARRISON[5]

REFLECTION AND DISCUSSION

When it comes to sexual integrity, what is your greatest struggle?

_____

_____

_____

What do you think is hindering revival from occurring in this country?

_____

_____

_____

Give three examples of sex without honor in our culture.

_____

_____

_____

Give examples of sexual compromise in the Church today.

_____

_____

_____

How could you influence others to model God's perspective on sex?

_____

_____

_____

What if we could simply _"Love each other as brothers and sisters"_
(1 Peter 3:8 NLT)? What would that look like?

_____

_____

_____

Chapter 3

EXCAVATION

Excavation: to excavate the scene and systematically remove debris in order to identify the possible origin.[1] In most restoration projects, it is important to remove all debris and get to the core of the structure you wish to restore. This often requires some deep digging. It is critical to build on a solid foundation. Without it, the renovation project will not stand the test of time.

"Therefore everyone who hears these words of mine and puts them into practice is like a wise man who built his house on the rock."

MATTHEW 7:24

REDISCOVERING OUR COMPASS

Imagine if you were in a reality show where you were dropped into an unfamiliar jungle and had to find a way out. If you were limited to only five extra items besides food and clothing, what would they be? Most survivalists would choose a compass. But this compass would need to be accurate and reliable. If not, it would do more harm than good.

As we view nature's world, there is an obvious sense of balance and incredible beauty. Most would admit that this could not have happened randomly. It gives us a picture of God's character and ultimately points to His benevolence. This is important because it helps reveal His attitude toward us as human beings, especially if we are lost. I think we could all use some help navigating through life's jungle. A compass could lead us to safety if it was accurate and reliable. God gave us the Bible to serve as our moral compass. God's character would not allow Him to give us something that would lead us astray. I trust the Bible because God has proven to be the most qualified person to lead my life.

As we seek clarity in a world full of moral confusion, we must address an alarming development. According to a recent Gallup Poll, the number of Christians who consider the Bible to be the infallible word of God have dropped precipitously.[2] Without a firm Biblical foundation, we can easily lose our way. In the words of Calvary Chapel founding pastor Chuck Smith, "If the Bible is not completely true or inerrant, then, pray tell, who decides which parts are true and which parts are not?"[3] In other words, if we can question and change what the Scriptures say, then we no longer have a standard.

Many today think the Bible is outdated and stands in the way of science, experience, and reason. But did Jesus view the Scriptures this way? From His early childhood, He studied the Scriptures. Throughout His earthly ministry, Jesus used the phrase, *"It is written,"* to authoritatively reference the Scriptures. I find it interesting that most people would say that Jesus possessed impeccable character. If that is true, then how could we think He would rely on and promote a flawed document containing half-truths, fables and made-up stories written by backward men from the desert?

I don't want to belabor the point, but if Jesus lived a perfect life and had perfect love for all of us, then His character would obligate Him to give us reliable truth that would stand the test of time. To do otherwise would be unloving, confusing, and cruel. The Apostle Paul recognized this when he said, *All Scripture is given by inspiration of God, and is profitable for doctrine, for reproof, for correction, for instruction in righteousness* (2 Timothy 3:16 NKJV).

The Bible is critical in giving us an understanding of who God is—what He thinks, what He feels, and how He works in the lives of humans. The Bible provides us with God's perspective. This gives us a moral foundation to face the challenges of today. We will not necessarily become rich or famous, but we will become wise. By reading the Word, we see the condition of our hearts, which leads us to make necessary changes (see James 1:22-25).

My goal is to read the Bible through at least once a year. I have been reading my Bible for over fifty years, so I've gone through the Scriptures dozens of times. It has never ceased to feed my soul and give me moral clarity. I can't imagine neglecting one of the greatest aids to life. It is such a treat and delight to listen to the Scriptures or dig into a favorite printed version. The question should not be, how much do I need to read today? Instead, it should be, how much can I read today?

Today we have several different versions, both audio and printed. I used to think that reading the Word was more beneficial than listening, but then I realized the early Church focused on listening to the Word (see 1 Timothy 4:13, Romans 10:17 and 1 Thessalonians 2:13). I've learned to go through the Bible one book at a time because that is the way God gave it to us. Each book has a primary point or purpose. Throughout the Scriptures there are major themes found in the various books—such as love, the Kingdom of God, humility, suffering, etc. I love finding these because I want what is important to God to be a priority in my life. I believe sexual integrity is one of these major themes.

One day the Lord spoke clearly to me, sharing an important principle regarding His Word. He said, "The more you read, the better you see." This is important when it comes to the subject of sex. As our society has become biblically illiterate, we are slipping into a myriad of unhealthy views of sex. Our moral compass ceases to be effective when personal feelings and current cultural trends become more important than what the Bible says. Fortunately, the Bible doesn't shrink back about sex or try to hide it in a closet.

The Bible is filled with sexual scandals. In Genesis alone there are five major ones: Sodom and Gomorrah, Lot and his two daughters, Dinah in Shechem, Judah and Tamar, and Joseph with Potiphar's wife. Throughout the Scriptures, we can see the blessings of following God's laws and the tragic consequences when we disobey them. As the wisemen were led by a star to the baby Jesus, so the Bible becomes our guiding star to lead us to Him. This is an eternal truth. *"Heaven and earth will pass away, but my words will never pass away"* (Matthew 24:35).

I consider myself more of a teacher than preacher. However, over the years, I have preached in various churches and ministries. Generally, I spend much more time in preparation for preaching than teaching. Occasionally, there have been times when the presence of God has come upon me, and it has given me enormous confidence. However, there have been numerous times when I have not sensed His presence. This has caused me to feel anxious and doubt my effectiveness.

One day the Lord gave me insight when I heard in my spirit, "Your confidence must not be based on My presence, but on My truth." It was a simple statement, but it had a profound impact on me. I love the presence of God and always will. When I sense His presence, I am filled with enthusiasm, hope, and confidence. However, His presence can often be fleeting and unpredictable. Too much dependence on our feelings can cause our lives to be unstable and insecure. But the truths found in God's Word are unshakable and unchanging. They can be trusted in all circumstances. As we trust in God's Word, we will be able to avoid the two extremes of arrogance and insecurity.

THE FEAR FACTOR

Today, there is another major theme found in Scripture that few are talking about. It is the fear of the Lord. The Scriptures tell us that Abraham feared the Lord (Genesis 22:12). It also tells us that he was a friend of God (James 2:23). I believe both are essential. The great Bible teacher, David Pawson, once said, "Our relationship with God must be both intimate and reverent."[4]

Years ago, I ran a coffee shop called the Urban Jungle in the heart of the city. It was located in a former adult video store. Most of our patrons were hard-core heroin addicts. They knew why we were there—it was to give them an opportunity to turn their lives around by surrendering to Christ. If, on occasion, one of our patrons swore loudly enough that others heard it, there would be a collective "Hey" by the others. Immediately, the offending party would say, "My bad," and cease his or her profanity. Even in those extreme situations, they had a respect for God.

Years later, I worked as a chaplain in a faith-based treatment center. It was in a former church. This program was thirteen months long—plenty of time to turn your life around. To my surprise, several of the clients engaged repeatedly in profanity. This always bothered me. Why did non-Christian heroin addicts show much more respect for God and the facilities dedicated to Him, than new believers who were constantly singing in a choir and sharing their testimonies?

Ever heard the old saying, "Familiarity breeds contempt?" It basically means that if you know a person or situation very well, you can easily lose respect for that person or become careless in that situation. I believe the street addicts knew their lives deserved the wrath of God. They weren't seeking justice from Him. They were hoping for mercy. To obtain it, they tried to show honor and respect to the people and places dedicated to God. On the other hand, most of the clients in the treatment program had heard teaching on the love and mercy of God countless times. Could it be that some had become so familiar with those truths that they had lost their fear of God and subsequent sense of reverence?

Now this demands a question. What is more damning, to curse and swear while in a fallen state of heart or mind, or to curse and swear after you have repeatedly experienced His love and mercy? Which person dishonors God more? Who is more guilty before Him? Because they prayed the Sinner's Prayer, some believed this obligated God to receive them into heaven. They falsely assumed they could continue to be undisciplined in their speech without subsequent repentance and still receive His saving grace and mercy. They thought their spiritual irreverence was just part of the sanctification process.

Christian author Trent Sheldon has insight on dealing with these situations. "The more chances you give someone, the less respect they'll start to have for you. They'll begin to ignore the standards that you've set because they'll know another chance will always be given. They're not afraid to lose you because they know no matter what, you won't walk away. They get comfortable with depending on your forgiveness. Never let a person get comfortable disrespecting you."[5] That's sound advice in human relationships, but I believe this also applies to God. People want God to be always affirming, but without His consequences, we quickly lose our fear and respect for Him.

When Moses and Aaron asked Pharoah to let God's people go, they were met with stubborn resistance. However, after the plague of hail, Pharoah appeared to have a change of heart. *"This time I have sinned," he said to them. "The Lord is in the right, and I and my people are in the wrong"* (Exodus 9:27). Moses sensed these words were hollow and insincere and confronted Pharoah. Moses boldly proclaimed, *"I know that you and your officials still do not fear the Lord God"* (Exodus 9:30). This proved to be at the heart of the matter. Without the fear of the Lord, our words can lack credibility and our actions expose insincerity.

The love of God is a common subject in Sunday morning sermons. What is uncommon is a message on the fear of the Lord. Today, we are getting a half-gospel. Jim Bakker was a famous television preacher in the 1980s who was caught in a sexual scandal. Later, he went to prison and was ostracized by most in the Church. But John Bevere, a national Christian leader, went to visit him in prison. At one point, John asked Jim, "When did you stop loving God?" Jim shocked John Bevere by saying, "I never stopped loving God. I stopped fearing God."[4]

When Moses was finally able to lead the children of Israel out of Egypt, he directed them to the base of Mt. Sinai. Moses wanted them to have a similar experience with God like he had through the burning bush. *When the people saw the thunder and lightning and heard the trumpet and saw the mountain in smoke, they trembled with fear. They stayed at a distance and said to Moses, "Speak to us yourself and we will listen. But do not have God speak to us or we will die." Moses said to the people, "Do not be afraid. God has come to test you, so that the **fear of God will be with you to keep you from sinning**"* (Exodus 20:18-20, *emphasis mine*). This test continues to be needed for all those who would sincerely follow the Lord in holiness.

In the book of Isaiah, we find the prophet receiving a fresh revelation of God. His response was, *In the year that King Uzziah died, I saw the Lord, high and exalted, seated on a throne; and the train of his robe filled the temple. Above him were seraphim, each with six wings:. . . At the sound of their voices the doorposts and thresholds shook and the temple was filled with smoke. **"Woe to me!" I cried. "I am ruined! For I am a man of unclean lips, and I live among a people of unclean lips, and my eyes have seen the King, the Lord Almighty"*** (Isaiah 6:1-2, 4-5, *emphasis mine*).

In the book of Ezekiel, we find another prophet receiving a revelation from God. His response was:. . . *high above on the throne was a figure like that of a man. I saw that from what appeared to be his waist up he looked like glowing metal, as if full of fire, and that from there down he looked like fire; and brilliant light surrounded him . . . This was the appearance of the likeness of the glory of the Lord. **When I saw it, I fell face down*** (Ezekiel 1:26–28, *emphasis mine*).

In the book of Revelation, the Apostle John encountered the glorified Son of God. *I turned around to see the voice that was speaking to me. And when I turned I saw seven golden lampstands, and among the lampstands was someone like a son of man, dressed in a robe reaching down to his feet and with a golden sash around his chest. The hair on his head was white like wool, as white as snow, and his eyes were like blazing fire. His feet were like bronze glowing in a furnace, and his voice was like the sound of rushing waters. In his right hand he held seven stars, and coming out of his mouth was a sharp, double-edged sword. His face was like the sun shining in all its brilliance.* **When I saw him, I fell at his feet as though dead** (Revelation 1:12-17, *emphasis mine*).

Job had become increasingly demanding and judgmental of his friends. God was also the object of his complaints until Job clearly saw the Lord. His response was, *"My ears had heard of you but now my eyes have seen you. Therefore* **I despise myself and repent in dust and ashes***"* (Job 42:5-6, *emphasis mine*).

Even the shepherds, on the night of Jesus birth, received a fresh revelation of God. *And there were shepherds living out in the fields nearby, keeping watch over their flocks at night. An angel of the Lord appeared to them,* **and the glory of the Lord shone around them, and they were terrified** (Luke 2:8-9, *emphasis mine*).

Isn't it interesting that in the Bible, when God revealed Himself to His people, their common reaction was fear and awe? Now, how does this compare to our modern Christianity? We may claim to be getting close to God, but why don't we respond to Him like those in the Bible?

GODLY FEAR LEADS TO OBEDIENCE

Ironically, the first mention of the fear of God in the Bible was in relationship to sexual sin. A foreign king was attracted to Sarah without knowing she was Abraham's wife. Abraham hid this fact for a reason. *And Abimelek asked Abraham, "What was your reason for doing this?" Abraham replied, "I said to myself, 'There is surely no fear of God in this place, and they will kill me because of my wife.'"* (Genesis 20:10–11). Abraham recognized that the king of Gerar did not possess sexual discipline because he lacked a fear of God.

This illustrates a critical point. Bible teacher, Zac Poonen states that it is "through sexual temptation, more than any other area, that God tests whether men fear Him or not." One time he asked the Lord, "Why didn't you let boys stay sexually innocent until they were twenty-five? Why do they develop sexual desires when they are thirteen or younger, when they are too young to get married?" The Lord responded, "Because I want them to conquer in the sexual area before they get married."[7] Perhaps this is why the Apostle Paul encouraged young Timothy to *Flee also youthful lusts; but pursue righteousness, faith, love, peace with those who call on the Lord out of a pure heart* (2 Timothy 2:22 NKJV).

A critical component in our spiritual development is the formation of sexual discipline. If it is not developed early, it will need to be established in a restorative manner later. "A life which has become out of control only comes back under control through the processes of God's discipline."[5] "Self-respect is the fruit of discipline; the sense of dignity grows with the ability to say no to oneself."[6]

It is important to realize that God isn't just interested in rescuing us from hell. He wants us to partner with Him in His great rescue mission of planet earth. For such a dangerous and perilous mission, it is critical that He can trust us. We must be on the same page as Him. For this to happen, God will put us through a rigorous training process to make sure we will operate according to His design and plans. He does this not only to fulfill His will, but to make us better.

We stop growing when we stop obeying. If He asks us to do something, and we partially obey or delay our obedience, we flounder in our spiritual growth. Why? Because disobedience gives the enemy a place in our hearts. *You used to live in sin, just like the rest of the world, obeying the devil—the commander of the powers in the unseen world. **He is the spirit at work in the hearts of those who refuse to obey God*** (Ephesians 2:2 NLT, *emphasis mine*). When you know that you must stop sleeping with others who are not your spouse, you will not grow if you disobey. Plain and simple. If there is something in your life that has become more important than godly obedience, God will not allow it to prosper. Something good will become bad if it becomes the primary focus of your heart.

I find it interesting that nature and the demonic realm always obeyed Jesus. Everything obeyed Jesus except humans. This includes not just the skeptics and His enemies, but often His chosen ones. In Scripture, God's people often prided themselves in their sacrifice for the Lord, but they weren't equally obedient. *"For day after day they seek me out; they seem eager to know my ways, as if they were a nation that does what is right and has not forsaken the commands of its God. They ask me for just decisions and seem eager for God to come near them. 'Why have we fasted,' they say, 'and you have not seen it? Why have we humbled ourselves, and you have not noticed?' "Yet on the day of your fasting, you do as you please"* (Isaiah 58:2-3).

Today, we have Christians who try to compensate for their disobedience with sacrifice. But there is no substitute. Larry Randolph said, "As the postmodern Church today, we take a lot of pride in hearing God, but we can't take a lot of credit for obeying God."[7] I believe there is a correlation between hearing God's voice and our willingness to obey. If we are not hearing God's voice, it could be because we haven't obeyed the last thing He told us to do. Obedience opens the door of communication with God.

THE BEAUTY OF REPENTANCE

Back in the '70s, I was fortunate to see and experience a major spiritual awakening in this country called the Jesus People Revolution. It was a powerful move of God that touched millions of people. My life was totally changed and continues to be greatly influenced by that experience. One of the hallmark signs of that movement and others like it was repentance. People were confessing deep and dark sins and turning from them. Many of these sins were sexual in nature. They wanted to be free, not just forgiven. They wanted to be pure in heart.

A hatred for sin will lead to true repentance. We will not only love what God loves, but we will hate what He hates. Yes, hate. The Bible says, **Abhor** *what is evil. Cling to what is good* (Romans 12:9 NKJV, *emphasis*

34

mine). This contrasts with counterfeit Christians who still are holding on to a sin and don't want to let go. Remember, God will not free you from something you are still holding on to.

I had the privilege of participating in another move of God in the '90s. While I was in Mexico, God's Spirit fell mightily upon a missionary family and their church. Later, this missionary sent me an update on the work of the Holy Spirit.

> It's Wednesday morning. I just got back from the prayer meeting. We had over thirty men. The fire continues to burn. It's taken a different turn. Last night a deep sense of conviction gripped my heart. It was as if the Holy Spirit was shining His light into my heart. Those hidden areas that seemed forever hidden were graciously exposed—attitudes, motives, and thoughts I had allowed into my heart. I felt my heart breaking within until the soothing freshness of His love was poured out. The healing water flowed, cleansing those deep hidden areas. Everything seemed brighter—the weight was gone. The touch of God was on me as a new worship began to flow. This morning, again, He was with us. His conviction fell and many began to be broken—heart attitudes began to be exposed. God dealt with us in the area of pride. How good to be broken by His love, and how different from when man tries to do that work.[8]

The last sentence has continued to challenge me over the years. We can try, with human effort, to reinforce biblical truths, but without the help of the Holy Spirit it will not have the desired effect. When we confess our sins from a place of humility and brokenness, God will heal and make us whole.

TRUE REPENTANCE

One of the most famous sex scandals in the Bible involved King David and Bathsheba. She was the wife of Uriah, one of David's mighty men. Uriah was loyal to the king and committed to the protection of David's throne. However, David decided not to go to war with his men (see 2 Samuel 11:1).

Rather, he chose to relax in his palace. This opened the king up to temptation. *One evening David got up from his bed and walked around on the roof of the palace. From the roof he saw a woman bathing. The woman was very beautiful, and David sent someone to find out about her. The man said, "She is Bathsheba, the daughter of Eliam and the wife of Uriah the Hittite." Then David sent messengers to get her. She came to him, and he slept with her* (2 Samuel 11:2-4).

After David yielded to his sexual impulses, he tried to cover up his adulterous affair by getting Uriah drunk and telling him to go home and sleep with his wife. King David had now become proud by thinking he could cover his sin. But Uriah refused to go home because his fellow soldiers were engaged in battle. David panicked and ordered Uriah to the front lines and secretly arranged for him to be abandoned and killed. Later, David's treachery was exposed by the prophet Nathan. As egregious as David's many sins were, he still found forgiveness because he repented with all his heart. He was not just remorseful; he made a conscience decision to completely turn away from his sins. Look at this portion of his prayer in Psalm 51:1-4.

> *Have mercy on me, O God, according to your unfailing love;*
> *according to your great compassion blot out my transgressions.*
> *Wash away all my iniquity and cleanse me from my sin.*
> *For I know my transgressions, and my sin is always before me.*
> *Against you, you only, have I sinned and done what is evil in your sight;*
> *so you are right in your verdict and justified when you judge.*

With a heavy dose of grace and affirmation, many churches attempt to encourage those who are struggling in their walk. "Love them into the Kingdom" is the preferred method. I believe in loving others, but let's not forsake the scriptural admonition, *One who conceals his wrongdoings will not prosper, But one who confesses and abandons them will find compassion* (Proverbs 28:13 NASB). It is not enough to affirm each other; we also need to confess, renounce and forsake our sins to find mercy. "Christians must learn how to hate sin without hating themselves."[9] If we do this according to God's Word, great deliverance and abundant joy will come.

The critical question we must tackle today is, how are we going to treat sexual sin? Are we conscious-stricken rebels seeking mercy, or hapless victims seeking justice? Was our ongoing sexual failures God's intended purpose and design for us? I believe the Scriptures are more than clear. Let's join King David in sincere and humble prayer. Despite our past failures, despite the ongoing temptations from the world and the devil, let's lay hold of God's amazing grace and abundant mercy.

REDISCOVERING HOLINESS

One of the most common excuses I hear for sexual sin is that it is so widespread that it cannot be avoided. Many rationalize a strategy of moderation as a reasonable compromise. Over 100 years ago, the great preacher and theologian, Charles Finney, said something profound regarding God's purpose for us.

> He (God) requires us to be holy because He cannot make us happy unless we will become holy. Our nature being what it is, it is forever impossible that we should be happy without being holy. God is happy, because he is holy; He knows that we exist under the same law of nature and necessity; hence His benevolence prompts nay compels him to use this necessary means of securing our happiness.[10]

Think about this for a moment. Finney is stating that without holiness, we cannot be truly happy. Why? Because if we are violating our conscience, we cannot be at peace with ourselves. Our conscience prevents us from true happiness. There is an internal conflict between what we know is right and how we are living. Some would say they have never been in that state of heart and mind, but Jesus came to set us free from those things that steal our happiness. Regardless of our past, God created us to live free of sexual sin. We will be tempted, but we were never designed or destined to fail forever in this area. *It is God's will that you should be sanctified: that you should avoid sexual immorality; that each of you should learn to control your own body in a way that is holy and honorable*, not in passionate lust like the pagans, who do not know God; and that in this matter no one *should wrong or take advantage of a brother or sister* (1 Thessalonians 4:3-6, *emphasis mine*).

Throughout the Bible, we see God encouraging and empowering His people to be holy. There is a genuine beauty found in holiness (see Psalm 29:2, 96:9 KJV; 1 Chronicles 16:29 KJV). However, in the past fifty years, the words "holy" and "holiness" have fallen out of favor in the Western Church, and that's probably an understatement. Our culture appears to commend personal integrity, which emphasizes our ethical conduct with others. What our culture is not commending is holiness, which emphasizes our moral conduct with God. People who dare to use the term have been labeled as legalists, oddballs, and worse. But this should not cause us to discount what is a major theme in Scripture. We have no right to minimize what God has emphasized. Integrity may keep you out of jail, but a lack of holiness will keep you out of heaven.

Because we have these promises, dear friends, let us cleanse ourselves from everything that can defile our body or spirit. And let us work toward complete holiness because we fear God (2 Corinthians 7:1 NLT).

Even before he made the world, God loved us and chose us in Christ to be holy and without fault in his eyes (Ephesians 1:4 NLT).

As obedient children, do not conform to the evil desires you had when you lived in ignorance. But just as he who called you is holy, so be holy in all you do; for it is written: "Be holy, because I am holy." Since you call on a Father who judges each person's work impartially, live out your time as foreigners here in reverent fear (1 Peter 1:14-17).

There was a time when I lived next door to a great holiness preacher named Leonard Ravenhill. In one of his messages, he asked a series of provocative questions.

"If I was to ask you tonight if you were saved? Do you say 'Yes, I am saved?' When? 'Oh, so and so preached, I got baptized and . . .'

Are you saved? What are you saved from, hell?

Are you saved from bitterness?

Are you saved from lust?

Are you saved from cheating?

Are you saved from lying?

Are you saved from bad manners?

Are you saved from rebellion against your parents?

Come on, what are you saved from?[11]

I believe Mr. Ravenhill makes a great point. We talk a lot about getting "saved," but that implies being saved from something. God wants us to be saved from the destructive power of sexual sin.

MODESTY LOST

Breaking free from the enemy's accusations should bring us into a state of humble confidence. It also should give us a greater appreciation for modesty. The word "modesty" comes from the Latin word *modestus*, which means "keeping within measure." Daniel Webster speaks of modesty as an act or series of acts, consisting in humble, unobtrusive deportment, as opposed to extreme boldness, forwardness, arrogance, presumption, audacity, or impudence.[12]

Years ago, I remember working late at a Christian ministry. Suddenly, an attractive single staff woman walked into my office and closed the door behind her. I immediately asked her to leave the door open. She asked, "Why, have you had a problem?"

My response was, "No, I don't want one."

She complied. Without modesty, the opportunities to stray morally will continue to increase. If we give the devil an inch, he will gladly take a mile.

I once attended a church in the urban core of a major city. During the service, some young praise dancers participated in a specific worship song. It was obvious they were talented, and the song was well choreographed. A young teenage dancer dressed in a long chiffon dress whirled around, revealing the back of her leather belt. On it was stamped the word "Sexy."

Perhaps she forgot the message while dressing quickly that morning. Perhaps it was someone else's belt. Or perhaps it reflected her moral values. Maybe she wanted to be a sexy worship dancer. But why would any Christian want to appear sexy to anyone other than their spouse? Why would we want to flirt like the world does? *Likewise also that women should adorn themselves in respectable apparel, with modesty and self-control, not with braided hair and gold or pearls or costly attire, but with what is proper for women who profess godliness—with good works* (1 Timothy 2:9-10 ESV).

A popular social media account, PreachersNSneakers, has questioned if pastors should grow wealthy through religion. People are wondering if shoes valued in the thousands of dollars are a sign of divine blessings, or just wallpaper to hide their appetite for worldly fame. To many, these Christian leaders appear to be celebrity wannabes. In their effort to become relevant to today's culture, they have become irrelevant because they are no longer demonstrating an alternative lifestyle. Today, it is critical we embrace the Bible as our standard and guide. In the words of William Booth, founder of the Salvation Army,

> "Will you join me in this consecration? Long years may yet be yours. The world is before you—God is on your side. Men, angels, and devils are everywhere speculating to your future—Humanity needs you. A great deal of religion around you is in a poor way, robbed of its strength by worldliness, sensuality, and unbelief. It is rapidly approaching a condition of respectable superficiality. So hurry to the rescue, lift up your heads, fix your eyes on the future, rise to your opportunities, the biggest and grandest and most pregnant with blessing of any that have come to anyone in these last days. Away with fear, trample hesitation and mediocrity under

your feet. Forget the failures of the past, leave them behind you, let the devil have them and having taken your stand then . . . on and on and still on."[13]

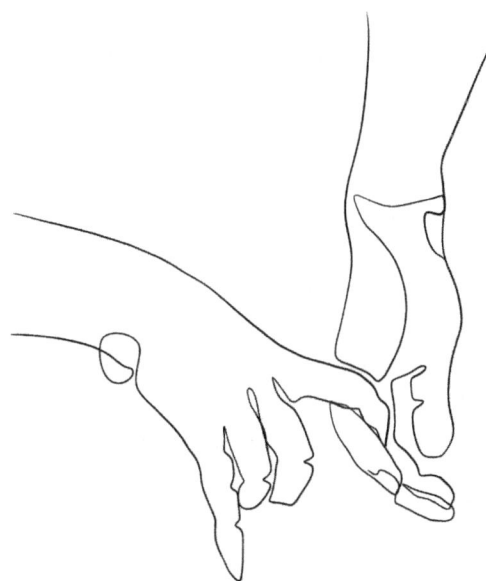

REFLECTION AND DISCUSSION

How often do you read your Bible? Do you have any Bible reading goals or plans?

_____

_____

_____

Do you believe the Western Church emphasizes the fear of the Lord sufficiently? Why or why not?

_____

_____

_____

Give examples of compensating disobedience with sacrifice.

_____

_____

_____

Why is repentance necessary for overcoming sexual sin?

_____

_____

_____

What is the difference between integrity and holiness?

_____

_____

_____

Why would a Christian want to appear sexy to anyone other than their spouse?

_____

_____

_____

Chapter 4

IMPLEMENTATION

Implementation: the process of putting a decision or plan into effect; execution.[1] In any restoration project, a plan of action needs to be devised after all the facts are considered. This plan must then be implemented for proper changes to occur.

Then the people hired masons and carpenters and bought cedar logs from the people of Tyre and Sidon, paying them with food, wine, and olive oil. The logs were brought down from the Lebanon mountains and floated along the coast of the Mediterranean Sea to Joppa, for King Cyrus had given permission for this. The construction of the Temple of God began in midspring, during the second year after they arrived in Jerusalem. The work force was made up of everyone who had returned from exile.

EZRA 3:7-8 NLT

In the book of Ezra, we see the terrible effects of the Babylonian capture of Jerusalem. *They set fire to the temple of the Lord, the royal palace and all the houses of Jerusalem. Every important building he burned down* (2 Kings 25:9). Many would suggest it was beyond repair, but God still had plans for the city and the Hebrew nation. To rebuild the temple, the Jewish exiles needed to engage in a massive restoration project. Once the plan was finalized, they had to carefully execute it. A plan without implementation is only a dream.

The story serves as a vivid metaphor of the God's redemptive plan after we have suffered the damaging effects of sexual sin. Through sexual sins, we often find ourselves in various stages of disrepair. However, God is relentless in His love for us. As we align our minds and hearts to His will, our temple will also be restored.

THE SURVEY SAYS

In chapter two, I mentioned a survey I conducted with a small group of Christian men. Another question I asked was, "What has helped you to overcome sexual temptations?" These are some of the answers I received.

1. I am still overcoming it. I pray about it and ask for help from God.

2. Staying grounded in prayer and Bible reading.

3. Learning ways to avoid these thoughts and shut them down when they come in.

4. Stay sober. Spending more time getting to know her.

5. Getting sober and not wanting to get laid by women as much.

6. Keep talking to the Lord and be careful with my eyes and not fantasizing about them.

7. Praying to God to help me.

8. God's direction in my life. Things haven't happened because He knows I haven't been obedient in my personal life.

9. The Word of God and prayer.

10. I have been trying to catch myself from saying things and not sleeping around.

BREAKING STRONGHOLDS

The word *"strongholds"* is mentioned in the New Testament and was used metaphorically to describe a Christian's spiritual battle: *For though we live in the world, we do not wage war as the world does. The weapons we fight with are not the weapons of the world. On the contrary, they have divine power to **demolish strongholds** (2 Corinthians 10:3-4, emphasis mine).*

In regard to sexual issues, it is important to discern demonic lies and worldly wisdom. There is a lot of information available today but much of it is not based on the Bible or a Christian worldview. I want to cover some of the more common questions Christians are asking.

• Is it okay to masturbate? What if I am just thinking about my spouse or girlfriend when I masturbate?

Most people hope there is some wiggle room here. I must admit I was one of those people. One day I asked God about it. He revealed to me that sexual fulfillment was never meant to be experienced separate from our spouse. In other words, God intended our spouse to be the only source of our sexual fulfillment—not anyone or anything else. Not even ourselves. This fosters trust between spouses and destroys sexual secrets and misdirected passions.

• Couldn't masturbation be considered a means of reducing our desire for porn?

What's the old adage? Two wrongs don't make a right. When I ran a coffee shop in the inner city, we served many hard-core heroin addicts. They would share their daily struggle of waking up sick each morning because of the drug working itself out of their system. In their minds, the only solution was getting heroin back into their bodies. At this stage, they weren't taking the drug for pleasure, they were taking it to feel closer to normal.

Ironically, this just drove them into a deeper dependency on the drug. They weren't getting free. I believe masturbation is used as a means of taking the edge off of our sexual urges. Like an addict taking heroin in the morning, it makes us feel more normal. However, we are becoming more and more addicted to it. We are being held in the web of sexual addiction.

• Will I always struggle with sexual lust?

It depends on how you define struggle. If you are asking if we will always need to be aware of the dangers of allowing our mind and passion to be led astray, I will say "yes," we need to remain vigilant. However, if you are asking if we will always fail in this area, I will say "no." This is not a sin that we are stuck with. God's grace and strength can transcend our weaknesses and set us free. I have seen it happen in others and experienced it myself. The Bible clearly teaches victory over sin, and we must accept this truth as God's will for our lives.

• Can I date a non-Christian?

Yes, but why would you? What is attracting you to that person? Is it their physical assets? Their glowing personality? These may be attractive qualities, but what is the spiritual condition of their heart? Does that person provoke you to love God more? I remember reading a dating tip one time: "Run as fast as you can towards God, and if someone keeps up with you, introduce yourself." I would start there. If the person doesn't inspire you to love God more, then they are a threat to your spiritual well-being.

• If I continue to fail in this area, does that mean I will lose my salvation?

First of all, when it comes to righteousness and judgment, the Bible states, *Will not the judge of all the earth do right?* (Genesis 18:25). We must never forget that God knows the true condition of our heart. As a judge, He is interested in motive and degree of premeditation, as well as our actions. In other words, He takes everything into consideration. *Therefore do not let sin **reign** in your mortal body so that you obey its evil desires* (Romans

6:12, *emphasis mine*). The Scriptures admonish us to not allow any sin to reign (rule) in our lives. It also reminds us to not continue in our sin (see Hebrews 10:26, 1 John 3:6). When we occasionally commit sexual sin, we can be restored if we quickly admit and humbly confess it to God. The danger lies when we sin and resign ourselves to continual failure in this area. This takes us outside of God's plan and purpose for our life. It is making peace with our sin, which can then become *sin that leads to death* (1 John 5:16-19).

REDIRECTING OUR HEARTS

Let me offer you some advice on turning from sexual temptation and embracing sexual integrity. If you see a dog chewing on a bone, don't try to rip it from his mouth. If you do, you might not like the results. The dog will probably resist, growl, and even bite your hand. Not recommended.

If you want a dog to drop his bone, try waving a steak in front of him. In most cases, the dog will let go to grab ahold of that steak. Do you see my point? Sexual lust is like a bone we chew on because we enjoy it. It tastes great, so we don't want anyone to take it away. But what if something even better was waved in front of us? What if it was so much better that we were able to forget about the bone?

Sexual lust is a very powerful desire. To defeat it, we must redirect our hearts towards God and His beautiful kingdom. The more we gaze on His majesty, the more we can ignore the shallow counterfeits for joy the world offers. In 1922, Helen Lemmel released the classic hymn, *Turn Your Eyes Upon Jesus*.[2] I particularly love the chorus.

Turn your eyes upon Jesus,

Look full in His wonderful face,

And the things of earth will grow strangely dim,

In the light of His glory and grace.

That's the key. I find when our hearts are directed in worship to God, sexual lust loses its power. That is because we are experiencing something so much more fulfilling and satisfying. There is great value in redirecting our attention from the things the world loves to those that have eternal value.

When alone in my car, I love to play worship music or an audio version of the Bible. At home, I constantly immerse myself in music, podcasts, and books that point me to my Lord and Savior. Sin seems stupid in His presence. When you cultivate an atmosphere where God is the focus, you experience moral clarity. Additionally, surround yourself with like-minded people who have a passion for God. There is a biblical concept of fire begetting fire and iron sharpening iron (see Proverbs 27:17). This way, one person can be used by God to help another Christian and it becomes mutually beneficial.

I love Nehemiah's response to the wicked men who were trying to distract him from his holy calling and purpose. *"I am doing a great work, so that I cannot come down"* (Nehemiah 6:3 KJV). Oh, that we would have that attitude throughout our lives! To be captivated by a greater love and a greater cause than what the world has to offer. I believe God wants us to focus on Him more than our sin. *Let us fix our eyes on Jesus, the author and perfecter of our faith* (Hebrews 12:2). He also wants us to intentionally limit what we watch and think about. *Finally, brothers and sisters, whatever is true, whatever is noble, whatever is right, whatever is pure, whatever is lovely, whatever is admirable—if anything is excellent or praiseworthy— think about such things* (Philippians 4:8).

POWER OF LOVE

I want you to consider the following words Jesus gave to His disciples nearing the end of His earthly ministry. *"If you love me, keep my commands"* (John 14:15). *"Whoever has my commands and keeps them is the one who loves me"* (John 14:21). Finally, *"Anyone who loves me will obey my teaching"* (John 14:23).

Isn't it obvious that loving God and obedience are interconnected? We lack the power and motivation to be sexually pure if we are not grounded in His love. The Apostle John said, *Loving God means keeping his commandments, and his commandments are not burdensome* (1 John 5:3). When we love God, his commandments regarding sexual purity aren't a burden. We simply embrace the wisdom and love He has for our life. *So I say, walk by the Spirit, and you will not gratify the desires of the flesh* (Galatians 5:16).

King Saul constantly treated God's commandments as suggestions or advice. He often sacrificed to compensate for his lack of obedience. When confronted, Saul justified or minimized the offense. This attitude led to his downfall. But here's the surprise: the Scriptures never said that Saul loved God. Many believers today seem content with being a servant of God but have no interest in intimacy with Him. They are comfortable with a distant relationship, assuming this will give them more freedom and control.

THIS LITTLE LIGHT OF MINE

Sexual lust seeks darkness and isolation. To defeat it, you must bring it into the light. One time I experienced a powerful move of God in Mexico. After several days of intense spiritual revival, I asked God what He wanted me to do once I returned to Minnesota. One of the things He said was, "I want you to be the same in private as you are in public." I knew what He meant. For some time, I had put on a facade that I was having victory with sexual sin. Only God knew of my struggles. I carried a secret fear that I would not be able to fulfill my spiritual destiny until this area was conquered in my life.

It came to a head one Sunday morning when my pastor encouraged all Christians to get right with God. Soon, I found myself down at the altar asking God to forgive me again and make me whole. Suddenly, I felt a tap on my shoulder. I looked around and a young man asked me, "Can I speak with you in private?" This seemed a bit unusual and awkward, but I complied. As we stepped into a private room, this young man began to share about his struggles with sexual sin, and asked if I would be willing to be an accountability partner with him. I knew this wasn't a coincidence. It was obviously a divine appointment and an answer to both of our prayers. So, I agreed, and we determined to meet once a week where we could honestly share our progress and/or struggles from the previous week.

With this commitment, I suddenly knew I would need to be much more intentional in overcoming sexual lust. No longer was I free to work at my own pace, with my own level of commitment. I knew in a week I would have my efforts brought to light for someone else to know. When we got together, we found ourselves at a level of transparency that was unprecedented for us. We were now fighting this battle together and refusing to hide behind our Christian reputation. It wasn't long before some other young men in the church discovered what steps we were taking to get clean and wanted to join us. Now we had a half-dozen young men meeting together and being the most open and honest we could possibly be.

We realized that for years, pride had kept us from victory. In the past, we tried to convey an image of Christian victory, which proved to be shallow and fake. We now wanted freedom more than faking our Christian testimony. We wanted to be authentic and true to God and to one another. I discovered that, when facing daily temptations, I knew that a compromise would bring consequences in the form of confession at the next meeting. I also knew I had to be honest with my failures because everyone else was. Amazingly, after saying "no" to temptation enough times, it slowly became a habit.

We met weekly for about two years. I can say without hesitation, our meetings broke the back of sexual sin and lust in us. What was once a private battle had become a united fight for sexual purity. To my knowledge, all of us experienced real, genuine breakthroughs. Looking back, I'm glad I didn't start with a close friend because that would have made it easier to fail. Amazingly, through the process we all reached a deeper level of love and respect for each other.

Besides personal benefits, I believe this was a great blessing for our wives and children. We had taken a much stronger spiritual position as husbands and fathers in our family. We sensed God's favor and support. Confidence began to arise, and a greater sense of fulfilling our spiritual calling emerged. Writing this book is an extension of this principle. The enemy wants us to fight a private battle. That will always be a weaker position. United we stand, divided we fall.

DON'T FEED THE TIGER!

Sexual lust is always hungry. But it can only hurt you if you feed it. One time, I was meditating on this subject, and I saw myself in a castle. This castle was protected by a large wall with a single gate to the outside. Inside this gate, there was a dangerous tiger tethered to the ground. Instinctively, I positioned myself far enough from him not to be eaten. However, this clearly hindered me from exiting the castle grounds.

This tiger was not only in a strategic position, but I could tell he was very hungry. From a safe distance, I could reach out and feed the tiger. Surprisingly, when I did this, the tiger instantly became larger. This made it even more difficult to leave. However, I also discovered that if I didn't feed the tiger, he would get noticeably smaller. This made escaping around him much more possible. It became clear to me that the tiger was sexual lust. It had positioned itself very strategically. If I wanted to go out and fulfill my spiritual destiny, I would have to get by the tiger. However, that would not be possible if I fed him.

There was a time when I would be more inclined to take a second look at some sexually provocative person or image. It could have been on the internet, a movie, or just someone in the grocery store. I would think, who would know? How could this hurt anyone? What's wrong with satisfying my curiosity?

Listen to what I am about to say, because your spiritual life may depend upon it. That second look to satisfy your curiosity will **NEVER** be good for you. It will always lead to a larger sexual hunger. If you feed the tiger, it will get bigger—guaranteed! Stop trying to justify the second look. Stop trying to excuse it. Just don't do it. You will never be helped by feeding the tiger.

I would take it a step further and challenge you to starve the secular aspects of your life. Sometimes we have to be drastic. This could be secular music, movies, or TikTok. Our constant exposure to these influences can lead to seductive nightmares and fantasies. We need to ask God to reveal anything in our life that is feeding the tiger. Fasting can be an effective tool in disciplining our flesh. *For we know that our old self was crucified with him so that the body ruled by sin might be done away with, that we should no longer be slaves to sin* (Romans 6:6).

FIGHT OR FLIGHT?

Surprisingly, the Bible doesn't tell us to fight sexual temptation. It commands us to run from it. *Flee from sexual immorality. All other sins a person commits are outside the body, but whoever sins sexually, sins against their own body* (1 Corinthians 6:18). To flee means to make a hasty exit from a dangerous situation. Remember, Joseph ran from Potipher's wife. He took the most effective measure for escaping the temptation. Why did he take this position? Because he regarded sexual sin as wickedness not as a weakness (see Genesis 39:9). Because of his fear of the Lord, Joseph determined to flee rather than flirt with adultery. *I discovered that a seductive woman is a trap more bitter than death. Her passion is a snare, and her soft hands are chains. Those who are pleasing to God will escape her, but sinners will be caught in her snare* (Ecclesiastes 7:26).

Joseph's situation was dramatic. He had to literally run from a woman who was doing everything she could to get him in bed with her. But those situations are rare. What is more common are the opportunities that come our way. It could be a concert, a wedding reception, or an R-rated movie. It could be an attractive coworker or a particular website. We know when our sexual urges are being aroused. It is at those times we need to flee before we fall prey. When faced with strong sexual temptations, look for the nearest exit door. Let's not forget that God has promised to make a way of escape. *No temptation has overtaken you except what is common to mankind. And God is faithful; he will not let you be tempted beyond what you can bear. But when you are tempted, he will also provide a way out so that you can endure it* (1 Corinthians 10:13).

Sexual sin is nothing to play with. We must turn off the computer. We must purge our cell phones of inappropriate content. *When the woman saw that the fruit of the tree was good for food and **pleasing to the eye**, and also* *desirable for gaining wisdom, she took some and ate it. She also gave some to her husband, who was with her, and he ate it* (Genesis 3:6 *emphasis mine*). Sexual sin is our tree in the Garden. Its allurement belies its hidden danger. Some things are better left alone. Even nature teaches us this.

What do the lionfish, the dart frog, and the blue-ringed octopus have in common? They are some of the most beautiful creatures in the world, but also some of the most deadly. Lionfish have eighteen venomous feathery spines along their backs and sides, which carry a deadly poison. Most frogs produce skin toxins, but the poison dart frogs from Central and South America are the most potent of all. The golden poison frog contains enough poison to kill ten people. Although the blue-ringed octopus is only the size of a golf ball, its venom is deadly. It can cause respiratory failure within ten minutes, and death within thirty. One bite can kill up to twenty-six men, and there is no antidote. The book of Proverbs warns us, *Good friend, follow your father's good advice; don't wander off from your mother's teachings . . . They'll protect you from promiscuous women, from the seductive talk of some temptress. Don't lustfully fantasize on her beauty, nor be taken in by her bedroom eyes. You can buy an hour with a prostitute for a loaf of bread, but a promiscuous woman may well eat you alive* (Proverbs 6:20, 24-26 MSG).

DELIVERANCE IN JESUS' NAME

Many who have struggled with sexual lust find the battle intensifies to the point where they cannot stop. Even when they try to flee, it keeps finding them. If you have taken steps to remove those things which have been triggering you sexually and are still oppressed, then there could be a demonic influence at work in your life. If you have suffered sexual abuse and cannot get free from the trauma, there may be a demonic stronghold holding you back. In these cases, you may need some form of spiritual deliverance. I would recommend getting with your pastor or other mature believers to pray over your situation. You could also pray a prayer something like the following:

"Father God, I thank you for saving me from destruction. I praise you for sending Jesus to die for my sins. Please forgive me for my sins against you. Specifically, I confess that I _____ (details of the sin). I repent of those sins and renounce it now. Lord, please purify my heart from this sin, the memory of it, and any associated fantasy I have entertained in my mind regarding it. In the name of Jesus Christ and by the power of his blood shed on the cross, I cut myself free from any harmful sexual connection that may have been established with _____ (name (s) or specific objects). Satan, I rebuke you in all your works and ways. I rebuke any evil spirits that have a foothold in me. In the name of Jesus, I command you evil spirits to leave me and go directly to Jesus Christ. Father, please heal my soul of any wounds resulting from these harmful connections. Please reintegrate any part of me that may have been detained through these sexual ties and restore me to wholeness. Thank you, Lord, for your healing power and your perfect love for me. May I glorify you with my life from this point forward. In Jesus' name, Amen."[3]

One of the more popular hymns I remember from my childhood was Power in the Blood. It seemed to capture the victory we are offered through Christ's sacrifice. I am so blessed that His blood never loses its power.

Power in the Blood

by Lewis E. Jones

Would you be free from the burden of sin?
There's pow'r in the blood, pow'r in the blood;
Would you o'er evil a victory win?
There's wonderful pow'r in the blood

Refrain:
There is pow'r, pow'r, wonder-working pow'r
In the blood of the Lamb;
There is pow'r, pow'r, wonder-working pow'r
In the precious blood of the Lamb.

Would you be free from your passion and pride?
There's pow'r in the blood, pow'r in the blood;
Come for a cleansing to Calvary's tide;
There's wonderful pow'r in the blood.

Would you be whiter, much whiter than snow?
There's pow'r in the blood, pow'r in the blood;
Sin-stains are lost in its life-giving flow;
There's wonderful pow'r in the blood.[4]

REFLECTION AND DISCUSSION

What has helped you to overcome sexual temptations?

_____

_____

_____

What questions about sex do you still struggle with?

_____

_____

_____

How can you redirect your heart to the Lord on a consistent basis

_____

_____

_____

How are you holding yourself accountable sexually?

_____

_____

_____

How have you "fed the tiger" in the past?

_____

_____

_____

Give an example of fleeing temptation in your life.

_____

_____

_____

Chapter 5

RESTORATION

Restoration: the act or process of returning something to its earlier good condition or position, or to its owner.[1] Eventually the hard work and planning begins to pay off. Improvements become evident and anticipation of a restored structure begins to grow.

With praise and thanksgiving they sang to the Lord:
'He is good; his love toward Israel endures forever.'
And all the people gave a great shout of praise to the Lord.
because the foundation of the house of the Lord was laid.

EZRA 3:11

RESTORING THE BEAUTY

One day, I was preparing to speak about sexual purity to a group of young Christian men. I knew many of these men had struggled with sexual sin in their past. They all wanted to be set free through a deeper relationship with Jesus Christ. Suddenly, something dropped into my spirit that I had never thought of before. The Lord said clearly, "I am restoring the beauty!" This was profound to me. I always knew of God's forgiving heart and a willingness to wash us clean. This, however, was beyond my current understanding.

What God seemed to be saying was that He was not satisfied with forgiveness of our sins. He wanted a restoration of innocence and a renewed perspective of sex. I saw He wanted to heal and restore—not just forgive. His goal is restoration. He wants us to be able to look at others the way He does. He wants us to enjoy sex the way He created it to be enjoyed.

This gave me tremendous hope for all those who forsake their old lifestyles and humbly submit to God. Many who have been caught up in sexual addictions have expressed doubts that they can ever find a godly spouse and raise a godly family. But now I see that it is not just a possibility, but it is God's design and desire for them.

IT HAS TO BE JOY

As a young Christian, I remember failing once in my battle with lust. I masturbated and I felt terrible. I quickly asked God for forgiveness but remained trapped in regret. In desperation, I asked God for a clear sign I was completely forgiven. I knew that Gideon in the Bible had used a fleece to gain clear direction from the Lord, so I sought to do the same. It was rather simple. I would open my Bible randomly, look away, and put my finger on the page. If my finger landed on the word "joy," I knew all was well. If it landed on the word "blood," I knew that something was still not right in God's eyes.

I did this with all sincerity, but my finger landed on some random word that was neither "joy" nor "blood." Disappointed but not discouraged, I told God that I would do it again, only with a small change. After placing my finger on the page, I would read five verses above and five verses below my finger. Whichever of the two words I came to first was God's direction. I was more determined than ever, but when I read this broader passage, neither the word "joy" or "blood" were in the ten verses. Now I was starting to panic. Could God be so upset that He was refusing to speak to me?

Just when I reached the height of hopelessness and fear, a biblical passage came into my spirit with unusual power. *If we confess our sins, he is faithful and just to forgive us our sins, and to cleanse us from all unrighteousness* (1 John 1:9). I was familiar with this passage, but it had never been made real to me like this moment. The passage left no doubt that by confessing my sin, God was faithful to forgive and cleanse me. The truth of this passage hit me with authority and power. My fears and doubts suddenly dissipated, while hope and joy flooded in.

I jumped up in my prayer closet, knowing my sins had been forgiven. The revelation had unlocked something holding me down. I was now set free. As I headed out the door, an audacious thought entered my mind. I boldly declared, "If I were to open my Bible, and place my finger randomly on any page, it would have to land on the word "joy." With complete confidence I then proceeded to do so. When I looked down on my Bible, there it was, my finger was on the word "joy." With a triumphant smile I said, "Take that devil!"

GUILT VS SHAME VS REGRET

I don't like to give the devil a double win. Consider how he operates. First, he persistently tempts us to sin, and then he demands that we give up because we've given in to his enticement. We are now twice defeated. When we sin, feelings often arise that can be overwhelming. Some of this is the guilt that comes from a sensitive conscience that has been violated. This is a gift from the Holy Spirit that is intended to drive us to true repentance and full restoration of our relationship with Him.

But there is also shame—that beats us up through the enemy's accusations of failure. There is no hope in shame because no solution is offered. The enemy will tell us we don't deserve God's mercy and we will never change or be good enough for God to love. To combat these lies, we must do what Jesus did. He reminded the enemy of what the Bible says. He chose to believe and trust in God's Word rather than the enemy's lies, His own feelings or circumstances.

Finally, there is a problem that is often overlooked. It is what I would describe as "spiritual regret," and it involves our own accusations against ourselves. It is holding onto disappointing memories that become stubborn stains in the fabric of our character. It is that nagging feeling that we can never live down our failures no matter how hard we try. Even though we have rejected the lies that produce shame, we engage in spiritual flagellation as a form of penitence. We constantly doubt if we have repented deeply enough to deserve God's full grace and forgiveness.

I believe this is what Peter experienced after he denied the Lord three times. The Bible says, *he went outside and wept bitterly* (Luke 22:62). Poignantly, three days later at the tomb, the angel instructed the women to tell the disciples and Peter that Jesus had risen (see Mark 16:7). This was a clear message of encouragement designed to restore hope back into Peter. We may get knocked down, but we can't stay down. *For a righteous man may fall seven times And rise again,* (Proverbs 24:16 NKJV). We must get up if we fall!

GOAL OF THE ENEMY

Shortly after I became a Christian, I felt led by the Holy Spirit to journal the spiritual insights and revelations I received from Him. My very first entry was over fifty years ago (March 1, 1973). Ironically, the entry was regarding our battle with regret and shame.

> One of the primary goals of the enemy is to change a positive attitude of a believer to a negative one. Sin seems stupid to one who has a positive attitude. But to someone who has a negative

attitude, it is often looked upon as a temporary pleasure. A Christian should never be so reliant upon his feelings that he has to resort to sin to please them. Show me a Christian who maintains a negative attitude, and I'll show you a Christian that is living by his feelings.

If the devil can bring the believer this far (to the point of sinning), then the next step is condemnation. Depression, far worse than in the beginning, results. Temptations to sin are fired away at the believer to the extent of him feeling he can no longer endure. The point is now reached where the believer realizes that unless God intervenes, he is sunk. He is forced to put his full hope in the Lord.

Finally, the spiritual eyes of the believer are shifted off of himself and placed on God. Suddenly the cloud that had blocked his understanding of God's purposes is lifted. The gospel that was once hidden is now brought forth through the glorious light of the Holy Spirit.

Positivity is the recipe for success, especially when coupled with hope. We cannot win on our will alone.

CAN WE FORGIVE OURSELVES?

Have you ever heard the advice, "You need to learn to forgive yourself"? Or have you heard someone say, "The hardest person to forgive is myself"? I believe people who say such things are sincere, but let's see if we can get some insight from the Scriptures.

In Paul's second letter to the Corinthians, he refers to his original letter and the church's former tolerance of sexual sin. In this letter, he clearly forgives them because they have repented. *Even if I caused you sorrow by my letter, I do not regret it. Though I did regret it—I see that my letter hurt you, but only for a little while—yet now I am happy, not because you were made sorry, but because your sorrow led you to repentance. For you became sorrowful as God intended and so were not harmed in any way by us. Godly sorrow brings repentance that leads to salvation and leaves no regret, but worldly sorrow brings death* (2 Corinthians 7:8-10).

The Corinthians had clearly seen their sin and repented with their whole hearts. Notice that Paul encouraged them to move forward from worldly sorrow to godly sorrow—to shift from self-condemnation to acceptance of God's forgiveness. "Forgiving yourself" may not be specifically mentioned in Scripture, but the concept of letting go of those things God has forgiven is certainly biblical. Anything else is condemning. Paul had to apply this spiritual principle to his own life.

> Paul, in many ways, set an example for all those who struggle to forgive themselves. He had been a violent persecutor of the church. But rather than live in shame and regret over what he had done, he determined to spread the gospel broadly. This was not from penance or trying to make up for his past. Rather, it was out of understanding God's great salvation. Paul writes, *Here is a trustworthy saying that deserves full acceptance: Christ Jesus came into the world to save sinners—of whom I am the worst. But for that very reason I was shown mercy so that in me, the worst of sinners, Christ Jesus might display his immense patience as an example for those who would believe in him and receive eternal life. Now to the King eternal, immortal, invisible, the only God, be honor and glory for ever and ever. Amen* (1 Timothy 1:15–17). Rather than refuse to forgive himself, Paul readily received God's forgiveness and rejoiced in it.[2]

Throughout the Apostle Paul's writings, we see that he was able to let go of his past and press forward because he clearly understood the power of God's forgiveness. *Not that I have already obtained all this, or have already arrived at my goal, but I press on to take hold of that for which Christ Jesus took hold of me. Brothers and sisters, I do not consider myself yet to have taken hold of it. But one thing I do:* **Forgetting what is behind** *and straining toward what is ahead, I press on toward the goal to win the prize for which God has called me heavenward in Christ Jesus* (Philippians 3:12-14, *emphasis mine*).

We are not the Judge of the universe, so we have no right to declare a punitive sentence upon ourselves. We need to humbly accept God's ruling on our lives. Forgiving ourselves ultimately comes from understanding

God's forgiveness. I'll never forget something my wife shared with me one day. "It was not his sin that kept Judas out of heaven. It was his perception of God." He didn't comprehend the extent of God's willingness to forgive sin for which a person has repented.

God offers freedom from guilt, shame, and regret. He also offers us a renewed hope and confidence – not in our own strength but in His. The Apostle Paul also understood shame and God's antidote for it. *That is why I am suffering as I am. Yet this is **no cause for shame**, because I know whom I have believed, and am convinced that he is able to guard what I have entrusted to him until that day* (2 Timothy 1:12, *emphasis mine*).

SEXUAL HEALING

The Bible says that Jesus came to set people free. He wants to free us from the nightmares of our past. He wants to free us from labels that people have put on us, or we have put on ourselves. God has great plans for us despite our past. With God there is always hope. Healing and restoration must involve letting go. A walking away from unforgiveness. We need to give our hurt to God so that it stops spilling over onto others. The story of the woman caught in adultery gives us insight of God's perspective.

> *But Jesus went to the Mount of Olives. At dawn he appeared again in the temple courts, where all the people gathered around him, and he sat down to teach them. The teachers of the law and the Pharisees brought in a woman caught in adultery. They made her stand before the group and said to Jesus, "Teacher, this woman was caught in the act of adultery. In the Law Moses commanded us to stone such women. Now what do you say?" They were using this question as a trap, in order to have a basis for accusing him.*
>
> *But Jesus bent down and started to write on the ground with his finger. When they kept on questioning him, he straightened up and said to them, "Let any one of you who is without sin be the first to throw a stone at her." Again he stooped down and wrote on the ground.*

At this, those who heard began to go away one at a time, the older ones first, until only Jesus was left, with the woman still standing there. Jesus straightened up and asked her, "Woman, where are they? Has no one condemned you?"

"No one, sir," she said. "Then neither do I condemn you," Jesus declared. "Go now and leave your life of sin" (John 8: 1-11).

The story gives a beautiful picture of what it looks like when mercy and justice come together. While the religious rulers didn't have room in their hearts for empathy, Jesus did. He reached out to her with love and gave her a sense of value and worth. He demonstrated compassion and spoke kindly to her. When no one was willing to defend her, Jesus put Himself between her and her accusers. It gave this shattered woman a different view of herself. She now had a reason for hope and healing. But Jesus did one more thing and it was important. He told the woman, *"Go now and leave your life of sin."* Jesus wanted the woman to know that God loved her, but she also needed to repent of her sinful ways. This is how healing comes. This is how true beauty can be restored!

Unfortunately, many Christians who have failed sexually feel abandoned by God's people. I remember reading a book entitled *Revival Lectures,* by Charles Finney. He was instrumental in leading our nation into revival in the early half of the 19th century. According to Finney's observations, revival changes the way Christians view sin in others. Christians stop scolding the conduct of those who have sinned. Instead, they become "sorrowful and tender-hearted, so that they can weep day and night."[3] Their prayers bleed with compassion and earnestness. It's been said about the great 19th-century evangelist D.L. Moody, that he was most qualified to preach about hell and the wrath of God because he did it with tears.[4]

BETRAYAL TRAUMA

Many men and women who are caught in some form of sexual addiction have experienced sexual abuse in their past. This has caused all kinds of psychological and spiritual difficulties. For instance, how hard would it be to convince someone that God is a loving father if they were sexually abused by their earthly father when they were young? It has been reported that "among men with mental illness, 40 percent report childhood sexual abuse."[5]

Recently, I have noticed people suffering from a phenomenon called "betrayal trauma." This occurs when the people or institutions on which a person depends for survival significantly violate that person's trust or well-being. Childhood physical, emotional, or sexual abuse perpetrated by a caregiver are examples of betrayal trauma.[6]

This is perhaps one of the most difficult forms of trauma. Besides the five stages of grief (denial, anger, bargaining, depression and acceptance), there can be an additional stage of obsession. "This is a stage where a person persists in thinking about the betrayal to the point where it becomes disruptive in their life . . . Betrayal trauma can have lasting effects, and recovery can take time. Sessions with a trauma-informed therapist can help a person work through the effects of their trauma and learn coping strategies to promote healing."[7]

PALMS OF HIS HANDS

God has placed us where we cannot be hidden or forgotten. It is a place where we can be clearly seen by Him. *"See, I have engraved you on the palms of my hands"* (Isaiah 49:16). Think about the implications of this verse. He cannot do things without being reminded of us. Charles Spurgeon provides additional insight, "I have engraved you." It does not say, "your name." The name is there, but that is not all: "I have engraved you." Consider the depth of this! "I have engraved your person, your image, your circumstances, your sins, your temptations, your weaknesses, your wants, your works; I have engraved you, everything about you, all that concerns you; I have put all of this together here."[8] We cannot be forgotten, and He will never leave or mistreat us. We can feel safe and secure in the palms of God's hands.

Earlier this year, I was meditating on validation, significance, and destiny.

It seems that these are all legitimate pursuits if we are doing it for the right reason. Validation from God is more important than from anyone else. I am amazed at all the people in Scripture that God validated. Overlooked and forgotten people like Hagar, David, Joseph, and the woman at the well. Even as He draws us to seek Him, it becomes a form of validation. Doing something of significance is also important to God but He wants us to measure it like He does. What the world sees as insignificant may be very significant to Him. Finally, we can't forget that our destiny is an eternal one. Our life on earth is but a dress rehearsal for what God plans to do with us in eternity. Our spiritual destiny must involve this eternal perspective.

He's Got the Whole World in His Hands

He's got the whole world in his hands. He's got the whole world in his hands. He's got the whole world in his hands. He's got the whole world in his hands.

He's got the little tiny baby in his hands. He's got the little tiny baby in his hands. He's got the little tiny baby in his hands. He's got the whole world in his hands.

He's got you and me, brother, in his hands. He's got you and me, brother, in his hands. He's got you and me, brother, in his hands. He's got the whole world in his hands.

He's got you and me, sister, in his hands. He's got you and me, sister, in his hands. He's got you and me, sister, in his hands. He's got the whole world in his hands.

He's got everybody here in his hands. He's got everybody here in his hands. He's got everybody here in his hands He's got the whole world in his hands.[9]

REFLECTION AND DISCUSSION

Have you struggled with shame or regret? Give an example.

_____

_____

_____

Have you had a difficult time forgiving yourself? How could a biblical perspective of God help?

_____

_____

_____

What was Jesus' attitude towards those caught in some form of sexual sin?

_____

_____

_____

What is the significance of being engraved in the palm of God's hand?

_____

_____

_____

What would be the challenges of accepting God as a loving Father, if you were sexually abused by a father or stepfather when you were young?

_____

_____

_____

Close your eyes and ask Jesus what He sees when He looks at you. What did He say?

_____

_____

_____

Chapter 6

REINFORCEMENT

Reinforcement: the act of making something stronger.[1]
To ensure safety and longevity, certain reinforcements are added
to restored structures. These reinforcements help to strengthen
and solidify all improvements.

The men in charge of the work were diligent,
and the repairs progressed under them.
They rebuilt the temple of God according to
its original design and reinforced it.

CHRONICLES 24:13

WHO ARE WE?

It is hard to have a productive discussion on sex without addressing our spiritual identity. We struggle more with lust when we lack a clear sense of identity. We need to know who we are and why God put us here. This is where the Word of God comes in. It helps answer these all-important questions. A client of mine recently said, "Coming into agreement with God regarding my spiritual destiny is critical to gaining motivation to turn from lust."

Perhaps we could start by picturing being in a beautiful tree house, in the middle of a lush forest, watching a bevy of deer frolicking below you. Next, imagine the most beautiful sunset, while sitting on a tropical beach with your best friend. Finally, imagine holding your newborn baby for the first time as they look lovingly into your eyes. How do these images make you feel? Peaceful, happy, content?

Now, picture God creating this vast universe. Billions of galaxies made up of trillions of stars surrounded by countless planets. Turn your attention to the planet where life exists in abundance. Here, God has taken the time to create the beautiful rose and splendid sunsets. He has made the magnificent peacock, the noble lion, and the splendid sailfish. All of creation speaks of the beauty, power, and majesty of its Creator.

Finally, imagine a lush garden where something unique and special exists amid all of nature's beauty. *Then the LORD God formed a man from the dust of the ground and breathed into his nostrils the breath of life, and the man became a living being* (Genesis 2:7). Notice that humans were the only thing in God's creation that were not created by His word, but only by His hands. This made it clear that He was willing to get His hands dirty for us. It is because He wanted to be more intimately involved in our creation and ongoing lives.

The Bible reveals that we were created in the image of God. A.W. Tozer exclaimed, "Nothing has ever been created that is more like God than us." Ephesians 2:10 (NLT) tells us, *We are God's masterpiece.* To know who we are we must begin with God. John Calvin once said, "Man never achieves a clear knowledge of himself unless he has first looked upon God's face."[2] This must be the basis for our identity. The early believers were called Christians because they thought and acted like Christ. They had come into a heart alignment with Him. This was their distinction. They didn't look and act like the world. They were different. This is God's goal for us. He wants us to be like Him. *And we, who with unveiled faces all reflect the Lord's glory* (2 Corinthians 3:18).

In the story of Pinocchio, Geppetto was a lonely old man, a woodcarver by trade. He had created many wonderful woodcarvings, but when he made Pinocchio, it was something very special. He wished upon a star that his puppet would become a real boy. Through the magic of the blue fairy, Pinocchio became alive. However, to become a real boy, he would have to prove himself to be brave, truthful, and unselfish. Through many trials and moral failures, Pinocchio's character was developed, and Geppetto's wish was finally granted. This allowed Geppetto to have the deepest and most personal relationship with Pinocchio. I see God desiring the same of us, but we must first turn away from our moral mischief and selfishness. God finds great pleasure in assisting us to grow and develop. Ultimately, this deepens and strengthens our friendship.

God's plans are not only wonderful but often mysterious. A baby in the womb has a limited understanding of themselves and the world around them. However, they do become familiar with the sound of their mother's voice. When they are finally born, they enter another world that is full of color, beauty, and opportunities. We assume this is our final destination, but it is not. Our current condition is but another womb that is preparing us for an even greater life. That life will have much more color, beauty, and opportunities than we can ever imagine. *For we know that when this earthly tent we live in is taken down (that is, when we die and leave this earthly body), we will have a house in heaven, an eternal body made for us by God himself and not by human hands. We grow weary in our present bodies, and we long to put on our heavenly bodies like new clothing* (2 Cor. 5:1-2 NLT).

For now, we must gain spiritual understanding and apply it to secure our final stage of development. The first womb was primarily for our physical formation. The second womb is primarily for our spiritual formation. Ironically, the key to success in our second womb is discerning the voice of our Father.

I find it fascinating that God created our necessities of life to be pleasurable. Food is necessary, but consider that each edible item carries a different taste, that we can discern and enjoy immensely. Sleep is also necessary, but it is enhanced through a sense of rest and peace. Creative dreams are also enjoyed during this state of tranquility. Sex is necessary for the continuation of our species. God could have given us the ability to engage in it without any pleasure, but that would not be true to His character. He is a giving God who is happy when His children are happy. Because of the immense satisfaction eating, sleeping, and sex can provide, there is always the potential of imbalance. It is critical that we stick with God's original design lest we develop an identity too strongly linked to one of them and suffer the natural and spiritual consequences.

Our identity should not be in eating, sleeping, or sex but in God and His Word. Our culture tries to convince us that our sexuality is the core of our identity. But "the Bible doesn't categorize humanity according to our sexual desires – or any other sort of desire."[2] "Therefore, when we make anything else the core of our being – especially our sexuality – it's not only a distortion of the *imago Dei* but also an affront to our Creator.[3] It is critical that our identity comes into alignment with God's original plans and purposes for our life. We need to listen to His voice, and put our trust in His will, because He is the most qualified to guide us to our final destination.

THE OLD MAN IN THE WOODS

What if you and two companions took a wilderness trip to Alaska? Everything was going great until, while on an extended hike, you got lost. At first, there is little fear, but that soon changes when darkness overtakes you. All three of you are then forced to spend an entire night in the cold, dark wilderness. The next morning you are hungry and tired. Throughout the day you walk but see no signs of your camp or civilization. Again, it is a cold, sleepless night. Hope and strength are fading fast.

Finally, on the third day, you come to a clearing where you see a small cabin with smoke rising from the chimney. This gives you hope that someone is there. Upon arriving, a kind, old gentleman steps out and greets you. He invites you in for a meal and a place to warm yourselves up. You quickly explain your dilemma and ask for help. The friendly, old man explains that he has no phone or transportation, but he would be happy to show you the way out. You respond with gratitude and anxiousness to begin the trek.

An hour or so into the journey, you notice the woods becoming thicker and the terrain becoming steeper. You begin to have some doubts about the direction you are going. You are also bothered by the pace of your journey. It seems far too slow. Finally, you express your doubts, but the old man tries to assure you that he knows where he is going and you're on a sustainable pace.

After several hours, you reach the end of your patience. You've become convinced the old man doesn't know where he is going, and that he's far too slow. At that point you and your companions leave him and go in another direction. After a day and half of arduous hiking, you come to a clearing where you see a small cabin with smoke rising from the chimney. You're back to where you started!

Now let me ask you, who's fault was your misfortune—yours or the old man? Was the old man unkind to tell you to follow him at the pace he recommended? Could the old man be trusted? He fed you. He went on the journey with you. Is God being unkind to tell us to follow Him at the pace He directs? Can He be trusted? He has fed you. He has gone on this journey with you. God is with you, and He is for you.

WILD HORSES

When Jesus entered into Jerusalem for the last time, He chose to ride an unbroken colt (see Mark 11:4-7). Normally, this would not be a wise choice. Apparently, Jesus' love was greater than the natural impulses of this young beast. Through this, Jesus was once again delivering an important spiritual lesson.

I hate to admit this but, in many respects, we are like wild horses. We can be immature, stubborn, and often driven by impulses. We have grown accustomed to fulfilling certain sexual desires, and we resist yielding to anyone attempting to limit or control us. Once captured, however, we must go through the process of trusting someone else with our lives. At first, we may be willing to accept the food and shelter offered, but not much beyond that. Most of us will gladly give God our sins. It's another thing to trust Him with our lives.

Hopefully, over time, we begin to yield more of our will. Jesus, who is caring and persistent, is breaking us and making us more useful. His goal is that we will not only be submitted to Him but enjoy partnering with Him. The Bible defines this as meekness. It is important to know that meekness is not the same as weakness. *Now the man Moses was very meek, above all the men which were upon the face of the earth* (Numbers 12:3 KJV). When Moses yielded his life to God, he did not lose his strength. He was never a weak man. He was a strong man submitted to someone he trusted.

I have read that in some rare cases, a deep bonding relationship can develop between a horse and rider. One expert described it this way:

> "Bonded" human/horse relationships are a step above the common situation. For both the horse and the human, these relationships tend to include varying degrees of appreciation, the capacity to forgive, camaraderie and the desire to behave cooperatively . . . To be part of this kind of relationship with a horse requires effort and a good deal of learned and developed skills on the part of the human. The horse and human are partners, each recognizing the other's skills and abilities. It is a pretty amazing and fulfilling relationship to have, and a badge of accomplishment for most horse people.[4]

To me, this epitomizes the connection God seeks to have with us. It may be rare, but it is what we were destined to experience – an inseparable bonding with our Master Rider.

ARE WE SAFE?

Years ago, there was a reality television series called "Pit Bulls and Parolees." It depicted the day-to-day operations of a rescue center staffed by former inmates who rehabilitated abused pit bulls. Ultimately, they sought to place the dogs in their "forever home" where everyone lived happily ever after. Often, the staff would visit a potential home and homeowners with the reformed Pit Bull. The dog was then put through a series of tests with other dogs, strangers, and small children to make certain everyone will be safe.

The question we must ask ourselves is the same. Are we safe? Do we pose any type of sexual threat to others? I'm not just talking about sexual harassment. I'm talking about our thoughts and intentions. Is a beautiful, shapely woman safe from our sensual, lustful desires? Can she trust us to not undress her in our minds? Can we consciously avoid connecting seductively with her eyes? Is our desire for God's favor stronger than our yearning to arouse her sexually?

NO COWARDS IN HEAVEN

Let's be honest. Many Christians today find it difficult to publicly endorse biblical standards. They don't like all the blowback that often comes. I'll admit to doing this myself. The danger is that it gives tacit approval to culturally accepted norms and can lead to moral compromise. We can slowly succumb to an "if you can't beat them, join them" mentality. It appears that many Christians have moral preferences, but they lack moral convictions. For them, Christianity is only a belief system, but it has not become a genuine lifestyle.

In Revelation 21:8 it states, *But the cowardly, the unbelieving, the vile, the murderers, the sexually immoral, those who practice magic arts, the idolaters and all liars—they will be consigned to the fiery lake of burning sulfur. This is the second death.* Sexual integrity requires great courage. It is not for the weak, and I am not claiming that it will be easy. It may be the most difficult thing you have ever accomplished. Like climbing a high mountain, you must not look back, but focus on the next step.

In our current culture, men of integrity are often regarded as weak. What we need today is more courageous faith in the face of adversity. Not shallow, lukewarm, impure faith, but the faith of the biblical prophets who stood strong in the face of compromise. Those who were more than willing to become enemies of the world to become a friend of Christ. "If the Christian faith is worth believing in at all, it is worth believing in heroically."
— Findlay[5]

THE CHRISTIAN LIFE

I believe the Christian life can be illustrated through a brief snippet of time in Jesus' life.

Then Jesus came from Galilee to the Jordan to be baptized by John. But John tried to deter him, saying, "I need to be baptized by you, and do you come to me?" Jesus replied, "Let it be so now; it is proper for us to do this to fulfill all righteousness." Then John consented.

As soon as Jesus was baptized, he went up out of the water. At that moment heaven was opened, and he saw the Spirit of God descending like a dove and alighting on him. And a voice from heaven said, "This is my Son, whom I love; with him I am well pleased."

Then Jesus was led by the Spirit into the wilderness to be tempted by the devil (Matthew 3:13- 4:1).

When the devil had finished all this tempting, he left him until an opportune time. Jesus returned to Galilee in the power of the Spirit, and news about him spread through the whole countryside...

All the people in the synagogue were furious when they heard this. They got up, drove him out of the town, and took him to the brow of the hill on which the town was built, in order to throw him off the cliff.

But he walked right through the crowd and went on his way . . .

*All the people were amazed and said to each other, "What words these are!
With authority and power, he gives orders to impure spirits and they come
out!" And the news about him spread throughout the surrounding area*
(Luke 4:13-14, 28-29, 36-37).

Based on this brief snapshot of Jesus' life, let's consider the overall results:

1. He humbled Himself.
2. The Father honored Him.
3. The devil attacked Him.
4. The Holy Spirit empowered Him.
5. The people rejected Him.
6. God rescued Him.
7. He spoke with authority.

Jesus has given a clear message to all His followers. *"Remember what I
told you: 'A servant is not greater than his master.' If they persecuted me,
they will persecute you also. If they obeyed my teaching, they will obey
yours also. They will treat you this way because of my name, for they do
not know the one who sent me"* (John 15:20-21). Based on this warning,
should we expect anything different? Although difficult, the Christian life
is filled with God's rescues, anointings, and victories. We must accept this
as our privilege and calling.

HOOK UP!

Years ago, I had an opportunity to go tuna fishing with five other friends.
We chartered a boat with a skipper and deckhand and sailed out of a San
Diego port to fish in Mexican waters. This particular year, El Nino was
bringing some unusually warm water north. Reports were that fishermen
were catching exotic fish, including the enormously large species of tuna
called bigeye.

The day was going just fine as we trolled for some tasty albacore. Suddenly,
the deckhand shouted, "**HOOK UP**," and the skipper immediately pulled
back on the throttle. My boss was handed the rod and encouraged to use

the chair equipped with a rod support and straps. This allowed for maximum leverage, which we soon discovered would be extremely helpful. The deckhand quickly assessed the fish was big. We could only hope it was a rare bigeye. As my boss fought the fish, it began to exhibit more and more the characteristics of that species. It is known to swim in a large circle around the boat. As it tires, the circles get smaller and smaller. The way it was fighting, we knew it would be a while before we could get it even close to the boat.

Finally, my boss had enough and gave the rod to one of my friends. He was a muscular, athletic football player, and put all his strength into it. The circles were getting smaller, but so was my friend's strength. Ultimately, he was forced to hand the rod to someone else. Minutes became hours and the skipper was getting more nervous. This fish needed to be landed.

The fish was finally beneath the boat but was refusing to come up. According to the skipper, he was thirty feet down in the thermocline region, where the water is oxygen rich. Finally, the skipper grabbed the pole to help bring him in. He was very skilled, determined, and strong. He pulled and pulled but he couldn't turn the fish's head upward. We had now fought the fish for over six hours and had travelled twenty-six miles since we first hooked up!

When it looked like we were at a stalemate with the fish, something finally happened. Suddenly, the line took off. Yards of it began to peel off the large reel. What on earth was going on? In less than thirty seconds the entire spool was stripped of line and then suddenly – silence – a silence that was deafening. Our fish was gone.

It was gone.

It was actually gone! Finally, someone asked the skipper what happened. With a sigh, he replied, "That's what happens when a 400-pound bigeye meets a 1200-pound hammerhead shark."

Later, I discovered the world record for bigeye tuna was 395 pounds!

Looking back, I have some regrets. One of them is that I never helped reel in the bigeye monster. Why? Because the rest of my fishing buddies and crew were bigger, stronger, more skilled and qualified than me. I wanted the fish landed, but I held back because of my fear of failure. If I could have overcome my fear, maybe the outcome would have been different.

What's the lesson? Sexual lust can be a monster. We can't be passive and hope it will all work out. We can't leave the fight for others to handle. We must be fully committed and fight alongside those who are equally committed. If we fail, we know we must live to fish another day. "Failure should be our teacher, not our undertaker. Failure is delay, not defeat. It is a temporary detour, not a dead end. Failure is something we can avoid only by saying nothing, doing nothing, and being nothing."[6]

CAN WE SWIM?

Francis Chan once gave a message entitled "Trust the Lord, He Will Sustain You."[7] In the message, Francis spoke of the inability to know if a person can swim if they have a lifejacket on. In other words, when equipped with a flotation device, you cannot tell swimmers from non-swimmers. Only when the life jacket is removed will it become obvious.

I once lead a discipleship class and had daily counseling sessions at a local faith-based treatment center. It was a wonderful ministry opportunity, but it was difficult to know how successful a client would be until after they graduated. When that occurred, it wasn't long before the client knew how well they could swim — spiritually.

In a similar way, many believers have benefited from Christian parents, friends, and a strong Bible-believing church or ministry. All of these are great blessings but there is a problem. Eventually, every Christian must personally know how to swim on their own. We cannot be artificially propped up for our entire life. I am all for supporting and loving one another. That is a major role of the Church. However, I am concerned about Christians sinking when they lose their support system. They appear to do well until they face a crisis in their lives. Maybe their pastor or mentor commits adultery. Maybe a Christian friend backslides, or a spouse dies.

These situations often reveal how well they can swim on their own. I believe we are only as strong as our relationship with God. It helps to have strong relationships with other Christians, but that is not enough. A deep, abiding connection with God is necessary for us to be able to swim on our own.

When I was in grade school, I remember taking swimming lessons at our public swimming beach. The classes were early in the morning when the water felt cold. I, along with my classmates, hated getting into that cold water. However, all of us benefitted from the training. The result? We don't fear the water and we don't worry about drowning because we have learned how to swim. You can tell the Christians who can swim by the way they act alone. They have a desire to serve God no matter how their co-workers live, no matter how their non-Christian family members act. They can be dropped into the most ungodly work environments, and yet they don't compromise sexually. They don't sink because they have learned to swim.

MAN UP

Be watchful, stand firm in the faith, act like men, be strong. Let all that you do be done in love (1 Corinthians 16:13-14 ESV). We need to revisit what it means to be a Christian. It is time we focus on our individual responsibility and conscience, rather than our individual rights and desires. That is the one thing we can do and must do. With that single decision, we become an influence for someone else to do the same thing. That's my only hope for real change. Dr. Ed Cole put it this way: "Maturity comes not with age, but with the acceptance of responsibility. You are only young once, but immaturity can last a lifetime!"[8]

This is going to take a lot of effort, but it is where the good news begins. What I've just said is entirely possible. Why? Because God is on your side. He is not only the ultimate healer and reconciler, but He is determined for you to reach all of your potential. Sexual sin is a hard taskmaster, and God is committed to making you victorious in every weak area of your life. Like a loving, dedicated earthly father, God's heart is for our very best. It reminds me of a poem by General Douglas MacArthur.

BUILD ME A SON

Build me a son, O Lord, who will be strong enough to know when he is weak and brave enough to face himself when he is afraid; one who will be proud and unbending in honest defeat, and humble and gentle in victory.

Build me a son whose wishes will not take the place of deeds; a son who will know Thee—and that to know himself is the foundation stone of knowledge.

Lead him, I pray, not in the path of ease and comfort, but under the stress and spur of difficulties and challenge. Here let him learn to stand up in the storm; here let him learn compassion for those who fail.

Build me a son whose heart will be clear, whose goal will be high, a son who will master himself before he seeks to master other men; one who will reach into the future, yet never forget the past.

And after all these things are his, add, I pray, enough of a sense of humor, so that he may always be serious, yet never take himself too seriously. Give him humility, so that he may always remember the simplicity of true greatness, the open mind of true wisdom, and the meekness of true strength.

Then I, his father, will dare to whisper, "I have not lived in vain."

—General Douglas MacArthur[9]

REFLECTION AND DISCUSSION

The chapter talks about wild stallions. What is the most difficult part of surrendering your will to God?

_____

_____

_____

Are people safe around you? How can you demonstrate this?

_____

_____

_____

How prone are you to sexual compromise?

_____

_____

_____

What is the most difficult challenge you have faced as a Christian? How has this affected your life?

_____

_____

_____

In what ways has fear hindered your spiritual walk?

_____

_____

_____

You find yourself in godless environment at work or in school. How do you respond?

_____

_____

_____

Chapter 7

FIREPROOFING

Fireproofing: rendering something (structures, materials, etc.) resistant to fire, or incombustible; or material for use in making anything fire-proof.[1] When restoring fire-damaged structures, steps should be taken to greatly reduce the risk of future fires. The aim is to provide sustained benefits for future generations.

Your kingdom is an everlasting kingdom,
and your dominion endures through all generations.
The Lord is trustworthy in all he promises
and faithful in all he does.

PSALMS 145:13

A LOVE STORY

I was nineteen when I had a dramatic encounter with Christ. As a result, I felt called to be a minister of the Gospel. I soon joined a Christian ministry located in Fresno, California. One of the requirements for joining was no dating for the first year. This was a shock to my hormonal system since I had lived a teenage lifestyle that always included a close relationship with a girl. I complied but found it difficult because there were some beautiful Christian women in the ministry.

One day I had an idea. Since I didn't sense God leading me to a life of singleness, but I was restrained by this ministry policy, why not ask God to withhold the revealing of His will regarding a girlfriend? In my mind, even if I knew God's choice for a mate, I couldn't do anything about it. I sensed that God honored my request. This enabled me to focus completely on deepening my relationship with Him. The plan worked wonderfully.

At the end of my first year, we had an international conference. Hundreds of godly women were attending this all-week event. God moved in a powerful way, and I felt drawn into a deeper relationship with Him. At the end of the week, I did something radical. I asked God to withhold His will regarding my love life for another year. Once again, I sensed God's approval, and experienced a more intimate relationship with Him than the year before.

At the end of my second year, we had another conference. Even though it was a powerful time with God, I didn't ask Him to delay again. Within a few months, I met a beautiful, godly woman named Martha. It wasn't long before we fell in love and got engaged. The rest is history. We have been happily married for forty-eight years! The irony is that Martha came into our ministry exactly one year after I did. Her first year coincided exactly with my second-year abstinence. It turned out that Martha could not have dated me during my second year regardless of my desires. Because of my willingness to wait, I believe I received God's best for my life.

MARTHA'S LETTERS

During our courtship, there were weeks when I was not able to see Martha. I was deeply involved in ministry that often took me to other parts of the country. The most common way we communicated was through letters. I've kept these love letters over the years, and I just wanted to share a couple of excerpts from Martha.

"Oh, that every day we might see a fresh revelation of Jesus, that our relationship might be changing and deepening with Him every day. Steve, I cry when I tell you that we owe our lives to Him—our very existence—and it's only the wisdom and goodness of God that we are together. I take nothing for granted and know that only through our continual seeking of His face can we remain as one. He would not allow us to do otherwise. And I know within my heart that we would not allow ourselves to be together if God were not pleased.

I want to be lost in Him, so, Steve, together we can show the world who God is and the depth of His love for His Bride, the Church. It's so exciting, Steve, for the greater I love Christ, the greater I love you.

I can only write to you when I so feel God has filled and inspired my heart, and now that I've had such sweet communion with Him—I write so that I might impart life unto you of which He's given me ..."

Yours – together in His Service
Love, Martha

"I feel ever so more challenged today to seek God. To know Him, then make Him known. That's my prayer continually for you—that your desire after God might welcome a consuming fire within you until all chaff is burnt away and all that's left is Christ, Himself to live and reign throughout us.

I'm so excited today to serve this great God of ours. The patience He has with us as He works day and night to complete the task that

He started within us the day we first saw Him as He is. Let us not look to the things behind but press on towards the goal of the high calling in Christ. It was so precious to me the night you told me you had determined in your heart to live as if we were married to the extent of taking on the responsibilities it holds . . .

I feel so much too, as one, to be united in mind, heart, purpose, and goal. As we grow closer towards Christ and are obedient to His commission – we will grow closer and closer to each other."

I love and pray for you always.

Yours,
Martha

This is the beauty I have been talking about. To be linked to someone spiritually, where both seek to please God in their relationship. I believe that is why we are still in love and have remained faithful to each other all these years. This was God's plan and intention for us, and I am so grateful for the outcome.

LIKE FATHER, LIKE SON

When my two children, Molly and Daniel, were born, I experienced anxiety, anticipation, and relief. I was present in the hospital for both of their births. In both cases, I wanted to make sure that my wife and our newborn were okay. Were they breathing on their own? Did they have ten fingers and toes? After confirming this, it wasn't long before I heard close family members say things like, "She's got her dad's dimple," or "He's got his daddy's smile." I must admit that I wasn't as perceptive as they were. To me, they just looked like newborns. However, it wasn't long before I noticed facial features and even personality traits that I could identify. This was very satisfying. It was like I was seeing a miniature of myself developing. It deepened my connection with them.

As they grew older, I enjoyed introducing them to things that I loved. Things like football, fishing, and knowing God. It was so fulfilling to see them enjoy the things that I loved. It formed an even deeper bond. We were now on the same page in many areas of our lives. We seemed to be able to encourage more excitement in the other person by simply talking about these areas of mutual interest. It was one of the most enjoyable aspects of fatherhood.

My daughter, Molly, got married, and with her family of three children, followed Martha and me into missionary service in Mexico. I was constantly amazed at the level of spiritual giftings Molly and her family exemplified during this season. It was one of the most thrilling aspects of missionary work for Martha and me. Meanwhile, God was drawing my son, Dan, into expanded ministry. First, he assisted me in running the Urban Jungle coffee shop in the urban core. Dan had won the trust of our patrons and poured his life into them. This opened doors for him to begin work at a local faith-based treatment center. Later, Martha and I joined him in ministering to these men.

I believe every child wants their father to be proud of them. They want to hear, "Well done." I can't imagine being prouder of my two children. I believe my ceiling has become their floor. As a parent becomes a grandparent, there begins to emerge a deeper sense of spiritual legacy and a desire to finish well. We want to solidify and pass on our biblical values and interests. Over time, a small tribe begins to form. I began to realize that this child-parent bonding is very similar to the relationship our heavenly Father seeks with us. He, like any parent, finds great joy and satisfaction in His child becoming a reflection of Himself. As our heavenly Father, He is thrilled when we embrace His interests and possess His values. Over time, He sees His children grow into a small tribe who reflect who He is.

FINDING OUR DESTINY

We know that God *created man in His own image* (Genesis 1:27). So, what is so special about being created in the image of God? Is it our moral understanding of right and wrong? Is it our ability to reflect certain character qualities? Is it our capacity to enjoy creative thought? All these characteristics are wonderful but consider this. Quite possibly the most amazing character–istic given to us by God is the power to create eternal beings!

God then gave us innate parental affections and the ability to instill divine wisdom in our offspring. We can form nuclear families that draw on His love and direction. The three members of the Godhead, who have always enjoyed perfect fellowship, are now able to extend this fellowship to humans. Think about this for a moment. Prior to our creation, only God experienced this connection, but now we are elevated into this level of parental affection and familial affirmation.

The angels don't experience this. Angels don't have fathers, mothers, children, or families. They don't experience parental bonding. They don't possess the hopes and fears that parents feel for their children. The angels have no way to relate to these deep family connections. They don't call God their Father. They don't focus on passing their interests and values to their offspring. Angels have one purpose; to facilitate the desires of the King. Fallen angels were not offered a redemptive plan to be restored to God. *Do you realize how fortunate you are? Angels would have given anything to be in on this!* (1 Peter 1:12 MSG).

Is it any wonder that the devil would try to distort, twist, and destroy this wonderful plan. Something this close to God's heart is going to get the full attention of the devil and his minions. Out of hatred for God, he has tried to disrupt God's plan for our families. He knows this will hurt God deeply, along with those suffering the consequences of sin in the home. But where the enemy has a plot, God has a plan.

OLD TESTAMENT PERSPECTIVE

What is the book of Genesis about? Perhaps you would point out the story of Creation. Maybe Noah and the Flood. You might even suggest Abraham and Sarah. Basically, Genesis is the story of a family—specifically four generations of a family. Throughout the book, we see this family display incredible acts of bravery and integrity. We also witness betrayal and suffering. We see God's plans and purposes fulfilled despite this family's weaknesses and failures.

The book of Proverbs is one of the most popular books in the Bible. For good reason. It contains wise counsel for everyone, especially young men. The truths revealed in this book are timeless and apply to all cultures and ethnic groups. It especially focuses on the dangers of getting involved sexually outside of marriage. In fact, this subject was a major theme in Solomon's writings, which also includes Song of Solomon and Ecclesiastes.

What I find interesting is the context. In the beginning of Proverbs, I get the strong impression that a middle-aged father wants a family that is built on virtue and wisdom. Throughout the book, the father is describing what hindrances to virtue and wisdom exist in this world. The most prominent hindrance is sexual immorality. Entire chapters are focused on this. The father wants a strong, honorable family. He wants to instill something that will help ensure blessings in future generations. This is what God wants. If our families are broken, or we are constantly buffeted by the shallow values of our current culture, we can find safety, strength, and rest in God's unshakable Kingdom.

Unfortunately, many of us have come from families that were filled with dysfunction and fragmentation. We live in a fallen world, made up of fallen communities that were formed by fallen families. What do we do if our childhood was filled with sexual abuse, neglect, and despair? How can we heal from these deep heart wounds and rediscover intimacy and affirmation? Most people desperately want to be loved, and God understands this. The problem is that many have made moral compromises to obtain it. Some people choose sex outside of marriage, hoping that it will be a temporary respite from the pain of loneliness.

NEW TESTAMENT PERSPECTIVE

If families are a critical part of God's plan for the human race, then why do some families experience barrenness? Why are some Christians experiencing a life of singleness? If Jesus was the physical representation of God, why was He single? Why didn't He get married and raise a family? Why were nearly half the books in the New Testament written by the Apostle Paul who remained a single man? Is it a coincidence that the two most impactful men in the New Testament were never married?

Singleness is not a curse or some form of imperfection. Perhaps Dennis Hollinger put it best. "Life without sexual intimacy and marriage is not a deficient life. Rather, life without intimacy with God in Christ is deficient"[2] We are in a unique season of our eternal existence, and our capacity for parenthood exists only for a brief time. "Rather than think of singleness as a temporary state before marriage, think of marriage as a temporary state before eternity."[3]

Jesus spoke of the importance of being born of the Spirit. *Jesus replied, "Very truly I tell you, no one can see the kingdom of God unless they are born again." "How can someone be born when they are old?" Nicodemus asked. "Surely they cannot enter a second time into their mother's womb to be born!" Jesus answered, "Very truly I tell you, no one can enter the kingdom of God unless they are born of water and the Spirit. Flesh gives birth to flesh, but the Spirit gives birth to spirit"* (John 3:3-6). Through these words, Jesus revealed God's plan for us to become part of a spiritual family that would bear spiritual children. In another instance, Jesus clearly prioritized becoming a member of this spiritual family. He stated to the crowd, *"Who is my mother, and who are my brothers?" Pointing to his disciples, he said, "Here are my mother and my brothers. For whoever does the will of my Father in heaven is my brother and sister and mother"* (Matthew 12:48-50).

Now, consider how the Apostle Paul viewed his calling and destiny. Although he was single physically, he was a parent spiritually. Paul called Timothy, *my son whom I love* (1 Corinthians 4:17) and Onesimus as *my son* (Philemon 10). He also called Titus *my true son in a common faith* (Titus 1:4) and referred to the Galatian Christians as *my dear children* (Galatians 4:19). Finally, Paul reminded the believers at Corinth, *I became your father through the gospel* (1 Corinthians 4:15).

When we look at the Old Testament, the emphasis is on marriage, family, and physical offspring. When we read the New Testament, the emphasis is on the family of God with a shift from physical offspring to spiritual offspring. The Bible is clear, whether we are single or married we all possess a spiritual destiny—to be part of a spiritual family and to bear spiritual children.

Jesus understood and embraced this spiritual destiny from an early age. When his parents found him in the temple at the age of twelve, His response was *"Why did you seek Me? Did you not know that I must be about My Father's business?"* (Luke 2:49 NKJV). This is so impressive. While others His age were struggling with puberty and sexual urges, Jesus was motivated by a spiritual calling that transcended the strongest of physical desires.

I believe this is a key to "restoring the beauty." When we focus on fulfilling our calling to give birth and raise spiritual children, our sexual urges become secondary. We become motivated by something beyond fulfilling our own physical desires. We realize that those entrusted to our spiritual care will be influenced by our ability or failure to discipline ourselves sexually. Many years ago, my daughter was struggling in her faith. One day, she was driving alone in her car, when God suddenly showed up. Among other things, He told her that He had given our family spiritual assignments that could not be fulfilled until she surrendered her life completely to Him. This was a revelation that completely redirected her life.

My mother passed away four years ago. She left an incredible legacy of love, mercy, and faithfulness. Of all her wonderful qualities, the greatest gift was instilling a sense of spiritual destiny in our family. She constantly encouraged us to seek the Lord and spread His love to others. She wanted every family member to be active in their faith. This was the most constant focus of her prayers. She was determined to see every family member surrendered to God, set apart for His service.

THE JOSEPH GENERATION

The story of Joseph in the book of Genesis is one the most fascinating and uplifting stories in the Bible. The story starts off by revealing what an extraordinary person he was. He was handsome, intelligent, and spiritually gifted. It seemed he had all the ingredients for success until tragedy struck. His jealous brothers hatched a plan to get rid of him. Yes, their hearts were so hard towards their brother that murder was a reasonable solution for them. Fortunately, that didn't happen, but he was sold into slavery to a traveling band of Midianite merchants. In order to hide their crime, the brothers then concocted a story of Joseph getting killed by wild animals. I think Joseph could have been the poster child for "betrayal trauma." I can't imagine the emotional wounds that occurred in his heart. It's hard to think of a more painful way to be betrayed than by your own blood brothers.

When we thought it couldn't get any worse for Joseph, it did. In Egypt, he became the slave of a wealthy family headed by Potipher. Without Potipher's awareness, his wife became infatuated with Joseph and tried to seduce him. He valiantly resisted her overtures until one fateful day when she literally grabbed him and wouldn't let him go unless he agreed to have sex with her. Fortunately, he didn't give in. He was able to break free and run out of the house. His refusal to give into her lusts created an emotional wound that spilled out in the form of hatred and rage. She falsely accused him of trying to rape her, and Joseph was immediately thrown into prison. Joseph's life was in shambles. Rejected by his brothers, caught up in a sexual scandal, and left to rot in a putrid dungeon.

But God.

The Bible does not suggest that Joseph languished in self-pity or plots of revenge. It doesn't say that he lost his sense of worth or destiny. Despite the circumstances, he remained faithful to God and was true to the small assignments God gave him, like helping the king's baker and butler. The Bible does not reveal the exact amount of time Joseph remained in prison, but it could have been as much as thirteen years. Regardless, he was released through a divinely orchestrated set of events. Not only that, but he was elevated to a place of authority and influence—the highest places in Pharoah's kingdom. Eventually, his brothers came to recognize the position God had placed their brother in, despite their evil actions. Ironically, the Bible doesn't reveal what happened to Potipher and his wife once they discovered Joseph was second-in-charge in Egypt. It doesn't tell us because it was no longer relevant. Joseph had moved into a new season, leaving that past season behind.

To me, this story is a message to those who have been caught up in a sexual sin and betrayal. It could be a tragic tale due to something we've done, or something done to us. Regardless, these situations leave deep emotional wounds. Often, we experience "betrayal trauma" because they involve people we have trusted. These experiences make it difficult to trust and love again. It leaves us feeling like damaged goods, with a loss of value that can never be recovered.

But God.

"We love until we are betrayed. Jesus continued to the cross, despite betrayal. We love until we are forsaken. Jesus loved through forsakenness. We love to a limit. Jesus loves to the end."[4] I believe God is working to restore the beauty in your life. This is what happened with Joseph. This is what happened with David. This is what happened with Hagar and Mary Magdalene. God is not finished writing your story. With Him, there is always hope and destiny. His promises are sure, His character without blemish, and His love without measure. Look at the cross one more time. Can you honestly say God doesn't care? Let His immeasurable kindness heal your wounded heart. Let Him restore your beauty so you can fulfill your spiritual destiny!

Charles Wesley, brother of John Wesley, the founder of the Methodist church, had a revelation of the power of the cross of Jesus Christ. Just consider the words of the song he wrote shortly after his conversion in 1738. We all, like Joseph in the dungeon, can be set free from sin and shame and walk in newness of life forever more. We have gone from ashes to beauty because of God's eternal love for us!

And Can It Be, That I Should Gain?

CHARLES WESLEY

And can it be that I should gain
An int'rest in the Savior's blood?
Died He for me, who caused His pain?
For me, who Him to death pursued?
Amazing love! how can it be
That Thou, my God, should die for me?

Long my imprisoned spirit lay
Fast bound in sin and nature's night;
Thine eye diffused a quick'ning ray,
I woke, the dungeon flamed with light;
My chains fell off, my heart was free;
I rose, went forth and followed Thee.

No condemnation now I dread;
Jesus, and all in Him is mine!
Alive in Him, my living Head,
And clothed in righteousness divine,
Bold I approach th'eternal throne,
And claim the crown, through Christ my own.[5]

REFLECTION AND DISCUSSION

What do you do if your childhood was filled with sexual abuse, neglect, and despair? How can you heal from these deep heart wounds and rediscover intimacy and affirmation?

_____

_____

_____

How can you overcome loneliness if you are single?

_____

_____

_____

Do you have children? How could you instill a sense of spiritual destiny in their lives?

_____

_____

_____

Are you engaged in birthing and raising spiritual children? In what ways?

_____

_____

_____

How could your success or failure in sexual purity influence others?

_____

_____

_____

How could the life of Joseph serve as a template for your Christan life?

_____

_____

_____

EPILOGUE

This past week I reached a personal milestone. I officially retired from my role as lead chaplain at a local treatment and recovery facility. In the past, I have worked with some amazing organizations. In the '70s and '80s, I worked with a revival ministry that focused on holiness. In the '90s and the first decade of this century, I worked with a mission organization whose people had a strong work ethic and served with incredible humility. In 2011, I became a chaplain at a drug treatment center. I worked with clients and staff who embraced honesty, openness, and vulnerability. It was so rewarding being around people who were genuine and real.

On one of my final days as a chaplain, I gave the clients a copy of one of my earlier books, Consuming Love. It just was an overwhelming feeling to see that my investment in others had borne fruit. Later, we had a retirement party with the staff where I was blessed to the point of embarrassment.

I couldn't help but think back on fifty-two years of full-time Christian ministry. Back to that initial encounter with God at Gospel Ranch. Back to when I first decided to sell my 454 Chevelle, break up with my girlfriend, and give my life completely to God. I chose a road less travelled by embracing repentance and a holiness lifestyle. But this has led me to see the value of humility, honesty, and a desire to finish well. In my later years, God has graciously directed me to pass on the spiritual insights and wisdom I gained along the way. That part has been particularly rewarding. I believe I can now die a happy man. They say you can't take it with you, but I'm not letting go of these precious things.

By God's grace, I now see the finish line.

ENDNOTES
CHAPTER 1: PYROMANIA

[1]See https://en.wikipedia.org/wiki/Pyromania#:~:text=Pyromania%20 is%20an%20impulse%20control,(pyr%2C%20'fire').

[2]Jonathan Cohen, Hear Buddy and Julie Miller's New Bob Dylan Co-Write 'Don't Make Her Cry', 2 August 2023, https://www.spin. com/2023/08/buddy-julie-miller-bob-dylan-cowrite/.

[3]Jonathan Cahn, *The Return of the Gods* (Lake Mary, FL: FrontLine, 2022), 80-81.

[4]Brie Stimson, 'NYC meteorologist fired a year ago over leaked images offers update on X: 'emotional and financial toll', 25 November 2023, https://www. foxnews.com/media/nyc-meteorologist-fired-leaked-explicit-images-leaves-social-media-emotional-financial-toll.

[5]Os Guinness, *Last Call for Liberty* (Downers Grove, IL: InterVarsity Press, 2018), 247-249.

[6]Sir John Glubb, *The Fate of Empires* (Hadlow Down, UK: Windmill Press, 2002), 8.

[7]Ibid., 16.

[8]Ibid., 17.

[9]Ibid., 19-20.

[10]Ibid., 21-24.

[11]Ibid., 27-29.

[12]Ibid., 24-25.

[13]Kirk Durston, 'J.D. Unwin and Why Sexual Morality May be Far More Important than You Ever Thought', 1 December 2020, https://www. kirkdurston.com/blog/unwin.

[14]John Stonestreet and Kasey Leander, 'No Civilization Without Restraint: Wise Words From 1939', 1 August 2022, https://www. breakpoint.org/no-civilization-without-restraint-wise-words-from-1939/.

[15]'Road rage woman burned to death by ramming rival motorist and revving her engine until car went up in flames', 22 September 2008, https://www.dailymail.co.uk/news/article-1059512/Road-rage-woman-burned-death-ramming-rival-motorist-revving-engine-car-went-flames.html.

[16]Elizabeth Grace Matthew, 'Review: The sexual revolution has hurt both men and women. Where do we go from here?' 15 December 2022, https://www.americamagazine.org/arts-culture/2022/12/15/review-louise-perry-sexual-revolution-244311.

[17]Louise Perry, *The Case Against the Sexual Revolution* (Cambridge, UK: Polity Press, 2022), 84.

[18]Ibid., 113.

[19]Ibid., 160.

[20]Ibid., vii.

[21]See https://www.firstthings.com/article/2023/10/we-are-repaganizing.

CHAPTER 2: SPIRITUAL ARSON

[1]See https://answers.justia.com/question/2023/08/03/what-is-negligent-arson-973952.

[2]See https://www.missionfrontiers.org/issue/article/15-mind-blowing-statistics-about-pornography-and-the-church.

[3]See https://thechristiantribune.com/christian-community-in-shock-from-pastor-tony-evans-stepping-down-following-confession-of-sin/.

[4]See https://www.pewresearch.org/short-reads/2020/08/31/half-of-u-s-christians-say-casual-sex-between-consenting-adults-is-sometimes-or-always-acceptable/#:~:text=Half%20of%20Christians%20say%20casual,is%20sometimes%20or%20always%20acceptable.

[5]Molly Harrison, 2004, Brooklyn Park, MN.

CHAPTER 3: EXCAVATION

[1]See https://aboutforensics.co.uk/fire-investigation/.

[2]See https://news.gallup.com/poll/394262/fewer-bible-literal-word-god.aspx.

[3]Rich Rogers, 'Why the American Idols Must Die', 5 September 2013, https://www.charismanews.com/opinion/40878-why-the-american-idols-must-die.

[4]See https://www.truthfollower.com/2015/09/the-more-chances-you-give-someone.html

[5]See https://pawsonbooks.com/pawsons-bible-study/week-8-genesis-part-6

[6]John Burton, 'Todd Bentley Scandal Reveals Bigger Problem: 2 Demonic Spirits Roam the Church Freely', 27 August 2019, https://www.charismanews.com/opinion/77758-todd-bentley-scandal-reveals-bigger-problem-2-demonic-spirits-roam-the-church-freely.

[7]See https://www.youtube.com/watch?v=1t0KjavbBn8

[8]Steve Gallagher, *At the Altar of Sexual Idolatry* (Dry Ridge, KY: Pure Life Ministries, [1986] 2007), 208.

[9]See https://www.brainyquote.com/quotes/abraham_joshua_heschel_114461.

[10]See https://www.youtube.com/watch?v=O_K7ppAhpmg&ab_channel=BethelI.

[11]Robert Duran, Steve Harrison, 3/31/93 Zacatecas Mexico.

[12]Christopher Yuan, *Holy Sexuality* (New York: Penguin Random House, 2001), xv.

[13]See https://www.gospeltruth.net/1857OE/570902_being_holy.htm.

[14]See https://www.sermonindex.net/modules/articles/index.php?view=article&aid=23311

[15]See https://webstersdictionary1828.com/Home?word=modesty.

[16]Cyril J. Barnes, *The Founder Speaks Again* (London, W.C., Salvationist Publishing and Supplies, Ltd, 1960), 165, 166.

CHAPTER 4: IMPLEMENTATION

[1]See https://www.techtarget.com/searchcustomerexperience/definition/implementation#:~:text=Implementation%20is%20the%20execution%20or,for%20something%20to%20actually%20happen.

[2]See https://hymnary.org/text/o_soul_are_you_weary_and_troubled.
[3]See https://www.missionariesofprayer.org/2010/11/prayer-cut-soul-ties/.

[4]See https://hymnary.org/text/would_you_be_free_from_the_burden_jones.

CHAPTER 5: RESTORATION

[1]See https://dictionary.cambridge.org/us/dictionary/english/restoration.

[2]See https://www.gotquestions.org/forgiving-yourself.html.

[3]Charles Finney, *Revival Lectures* (Old Tappan, New Jersey: Fleming H. Revell Company), 23.

[4]Christopher Yuan, *Holy Sexuality* (New York: Penguin Random House, 2001), 35.

[5]Diane Langberg, *Suffering and the Heart of God: How Trauma Destroys and Christ Restores* (Greensboro, NC: New Growth Press, 2015), 270.

[6]See https://dynamic.uoregon.edu/jjf/defineBT.html#:~:text=From%20Freyd%20(2008)%3A%20Betrayal,are%20examples%20of%20betrayal%20trauma.

[7]See https://www.medicalnewstoday.com/articles/betrayal-trauma.

[8]https://www.truthforlife.org/devotionals/spurgeon/11/7/2015/

[9]See https://www.classical-music.com/articles/hes-got-the-whole-world-in-his-hands-lyrics.

CHAPTER 6: REINFORCEMENT

[1]See https://dictionary.cambridge.org/us/dictionary/english/reinforcement.

[2]See https://quotefancy.com/quote/1118873/John-Calvin-It-is-certain-that-man-never-achieves-a-clear-knowledge-of-himself-unless-he

[3]Christopher Yuan, *Holy Sexuality* (New York: Penguin Random House, 2001), 47.

[4]Ibid., 17.

[5]See https://www.quora.com/Do-horses-form-attachments-to-specific-individuals-or-do-they-show-equal-affection-towards-everyone-regardless-of-time-spent-with-them.

[6]See https://disciple365.org/2013/12/26/disciple-of-christ-all-or-nothing/

[7]See https://www.forbes.com/sites/ekaterinawalter/2013/12/30/30-powerful-quotes-on-failure/?sh=5b104b2624bd.

[8]https://www.youtube.com/watch?v=yCwph3QvGM8&ab_channel=FrancisChanNetwork.

[9]See https://quotefancy.com/quote/799239/Edwin-Louis-Cole-Maturity-comes-not-with-age-but-with-the-acceptance-of-responsibility.

[10]See https://www.christianpost.com/news/tom-brady-shares-general-macarthur-prayer-build-me-a-son-o-lord.html.

CHAPTER 7: FIREPROOFING

[1]See https://en.wikipedia.org/wiki/Fireproofing.

[2]Christopher Yuan, *Holy Sexuality* (New York: Penguin Random House, 2001), 98.

[3]Ibid., 110.

[4]Dane Ortlund, *Gentle and Lowly: The Heart of Christ for Sinners and Sufferers* (Wheaton, IL: Crossway, 2020), 198.

[5]See https://hymnary.org/text/and_can_it_be_that_i_should_gain

ABOUT THE AUTHOR

Steve Harrison has been an incurable revivalist for over 50 years. Saved during the Jesus Revolution and caught up in a Mexican revival in the mid '90s, he has been forever ruined by God in a good way. He and his wife, Martha, live in the Brainerd Lakes Area of Minnesota where they often host their growing grandchildren. Steve continues to serve the Body of Christ as a scribe of God's heart.

For More Information

Steve Harrison

c/o Bethany Urban Development

P.O. Box 320

Brainerd, MN 56401

Phone: 612-598-3270

budministries@gmail.com